Highway Code
FOR DRIVERS

D0301195

© Haynes Publishing 2012

Pages 4–129 reproduced from *The Official Highway Code*. Department for Transport and Driving Standards Agency © Crown Copyright 2011. Reproduced under the terms of the Click-Use Licence.

First published in February 2012

A catalogue record for this book is available from the British Library

ISBN 978 0 85733 151 9

Published by Haynes Publishing,
Sparkford, Yeovil, Somerset BA22 7JJ, UK

Tel: +44 (0)1963 442030 Fax: +44 (0)1963 440001
E-mail: sales@haynes.co.uk
Website: www.haynes.co.uk

Haynes North America, Inc.,
861 Lawrence Drive, Newbury Park,
California 91320, USA

Printed in the USA by Odcombe Press LP,
1299 Bridgestone Parkway, La Vergne, TN 37086

This Highway Code applies to England, Scotland and Wales. *The Highway Code* is essential reading for everyone. The most vulnerable road users are pedestrians, particularly children, older or disabled people, cyclists, motorcyclists and horse riders. It is important that all road users are aware of the Code and are considerate towards each other. This applies to pedestrians as much as to drivers and riders.

Many of the rules in the Code are legal requirements, and if you disobey these rules you are committing a criminal offence. You may be fined, given penalty points on your licence or be disqualified from driving. In the most serious cases you may be sent to prison. Such rules are identified by the use of the words **'MUST/MUST NOT'**. In addition, the rule includes an abbreviated reference to the legislation which creates the offence. An explanation of the abbreviations is on page 118.

Although failure to comply with the other rules of the Code will not, in itself, cause a person to be prosecuted, *The Highway Code* may be used in evidence in any court proceedings under the Traffic Acts (see page 118) to establish liability. This includes rules which use advisory wording such as 'should/should not' or 'do/do not'.

Knowing and applying the rules contained in *The Highway Code* could significantly reduce road casualties. Cutting the number of deaths and injuries that occur on our roads every day is a responsibility we all share. *The Highway Code* can help us discharge that responsibility. Further information on driving/riding techniques can be found in 'The Official DSA Guide to Driving – the essential skills' and 'The Official DSA Guide to Riding – the essential skills'.

General guidance

1 **Pavements** (including any path along the side of a road) should be used if provided. Where possible, avoid being next to the kerb with your back to the traffic. If you have to step into the road, look both ways first. Always show due care and consideration for others.

2 **If there is no pavement,** keep to the right-hand side of the road so that you can see oncoming traffic. You should take extra care and

⊃ be prepared to walk in single file, especially on narrow roads or in poor light
⊃ keep close to the side of the road.

It may be safer to cross the road well before a sharp right-hand bend so that oncoming traffic has a better chance of seeing you. Cross back after the bend.

3 **Help other road users to see you.** Wear or carry something light-coloured, bright or fluorescent in poor daylight conditions. When it is dark, use reflective materials (e.g. armbands, sashes, waistcoats, jackets, footwear), which can be seen by drivers using headlights up to three times as far away as non-reflective materials.

Rule 3 – *Help yourself to be seen*

4 **Young children** should not be out alone on the pavement or road (see Rule 7). When taking children out, keep between them and the traffic and hold their hands firmly. Strap very young children into push-chairs or use reins. When pushing a young child in a buggy, do not push the buggy into the road when checking to see if it is clear to cross, particularly from between parked vehicles.

5 **Organised walks.** Large groups of people walking together should use a pavement if available; if one is not, they should keep to the left. Look-outs should be positioned at the front and back of the group, and they should wear fluorescent clothes in daylight and reflective clothes in the dark. At night, the look-out in front should show a white light and the one at the back a red light. People on the outside of large groups should also carry lights and wear reflective clothing.

6 **Motorways.** Pedestrians **MUST NOT** be on motorways or slip roads except in an emergency (see Rules 271 and 275).
Laws RTRA sect 17, MT(E&W)R 1982 as amended, reg 15(1)(b) & MT(S)R reg 13

Crossing the road

7 **The Green Cross Code.** The advice given below on crossing the road is for all pedestrians. Children should be taught the Code and should not be allowed out alone until they can understand and use it properly. The age when they can do this is different for each child. Many children cannot judge how fast vehicles are going or how far away they are. Children learn by example, so parents and carers should always use the Code in full when out with their children. They are responsible for deciding at what age children can use it safely by themselves.

A First find a safe place to cross and where there is space to reach the pavement on the other side. Where there is a crossing nearby, use it. It is safer to cross using a subway, a footbridge, an island, a zebra, pelican, toucan or puffin crossing, or where there is a crossing point controlled by a police officer, a school crossing patrol or a traffic warden. Otherwise choose a place where you can see clearly in all directions. Try to avoid crossing between parked cars (see Rule 14), on a blind bend, or close to the brow of a hill. Move to a space where drivers and riders can see you clearly. Do not cross the road diagonally.

Rule 7 – Look all around and listen for traffic before crossing

B Stop just before you get to the kerb, where you can see if anything is coming. Do not get too close to the traffic. If there's no pavement, keep back from the edge of the road but make sure you can still see approaching traffic.

C Look all around for traffic and listen. Traffic could come from any direction. Listen as well, because you can sometimes hear traffic before you see it.

D If traffic is coming, let it pass. Look all around again and listen. Do not cross until there is a safe gap in the traffic and you are certain that there is plenty of time. Remember, even if traffic is a long way off, it may be approaching very quickly.

E When it is safe, go straight across the road – do not run. Keep looking and listening for traffic while you cross, in case there is any traffic you did not see, or in case other traffic appears suddenly. Look out for cyclists and motorcyclists travelling between lanes of traffic. Do not walk diagonally across the road.

8 **At a junction.** When crossing the road, look out for traffic turning into the road, especially from behind you. If you have started crossing and traffic wants to turn into the road, you have priority and they should give way (see Rule 170).

9   **Pedestrian Safety Barriers.** Where there are barriers, cross the road only at the gaps provided for pedestrians. Do not climb over the barriers or walk between them and the road.

10   **Tactile paving.** Raised surfaces that can be felt underfoot provide warning and guidance to blind or partially sighted people. The most common surfaces are a series of raised studs, which are used at crossing points with a dropped kerb, or a series of rounded raised bars which are used at level crossings, at the top and bottom of steps and at some other hazards.

11   **One-way streets.** Check which way the traffic is moving. Do not cross until it is safe to do so without stopping. Bus and cycle lanes may operate in the opposite direction to the rest of the traffic.

12   **Bus and cycle lanes.** Take care when crossing these lanes as traffic may be moving faster than in the other lanes, or against the flow of traffic.

13   **Routes shared with cyclists.** Some cycle tracks run alongside footpaths or pavements, using a segregating feature to separate cyclists from people on foot. Segregated routes may also incorporate short lengths of tactile paving to help visually impaired people stay on the correct side. On the pedestrian side this will comprise a series of flat-topped bars running across the direction of travel (ladder pattern). On the cyclist side the same bars are orientated in the direction of travel (tramline pattern). Not all routes which are shared with cyclists are segregated. Take extra care where this is so (see Rule 62).

14   **Parked vehicles.** If you have to cross between parked vehicles, use the outside edges of the vehicles as if they were the kerb. Stop there and make sure you can see all around and that the traffic can see you. Make sure there is a gap between any parked vehicles on the other side, so you can reach the pavement. Never cross the road in front of, or behind, any vehicle with its engine running, especially a large vehicle, as the driver may not be able to see you.

15   **Reversing vehicles.** Never cross behind a vehicle which is reversing, showing white reversing lights or sounding a warning.

16 **Moving vehicles.** You **MUST NOT** get onto or hold onto a moving vehicle.
Law RTA 1988 sect 26

17 **At night.** Wear something reflective to make it easier for others to see you (see Rule 3). If there is no pedestrian crossing nearby, cross the road near a street light so that traffic can see you more easily.

Crossings

18 **At all crossings.** When using any type of crossing you should

- ⊙ always check that the traffic has stopped before you start to cross or push a pram onto a crossing
- ⊙ always cross between the studs or over the zebra markings. Do not cross at the side of the crossing or on the zig-zag lines, as it can be dangerous.

You **MUST NOT** loiter on any type of crossing.
Laws ZPPPCRGD reg 19 & RTRA sect 25(5)

19 **Zebra crossings.** Give traffic plenty of time to see you and to stop before you start to cross. Vehicles will need more time when the road is slippery. Wait until traffic has stopped from both directions or the road is clear before crossing. Remember that traffic does not have to stop until someone has moved onto the crossing. Keep looking both ways, and listening, in case a driver or rider has not seen you and attempts to overtake a vehicle that has stopped.

***Rule 19** – Zebra crossings have flashing beacons*

20 Where there is an island in the middle of a zebra crossing, wait on the island and follow Rule 19 before you cross the second half of the road – it is a separate crossing.

Rule 20 – *Zebra crossings with a central island are two separate crossings*

21 **At traffic lights.** There may be special signals for pedestrians. You should only start to cross the road when the green figure shows. If you have started to cross the road and the green figure goes out, you should still have time to reach the other side, but do not delay. If no pedestrian signals have been provided, watch carefully and do not cross until the traffic lights are red and the traffic has stopped. Keep looking and check for traffic that may be turning the corner. Remember that traffic lights may let traffic move in some lanes while traffic in other lanes has stopped.

Rule 21 – *At traffic lights, puffin and pelican crossings*
* *At pelican crossings only*

22 **Pelican crossings.** These are signal-controlled crossings operated by pedestrians. Push the control button to activate the traffic signals. When the red figure shows, do not cross. When a steady green figure shows, check the traffic has stopped then cross with care. When the green figure begins to flash you should not start to cross. If you have already started you should have time to finish crossing safely.

23 **Puffin crossings** differ from pelican crossings as the red and green figures are above the control box on your side of the road and there is no flashing green figure phase. Press the button and wait for the green figure to show.

24 When the road is congested, traffic on your side of the road may be forced to stop even though their lights are green. Traffic may still be moving on the other side of the road, so press the button and wait for the signal to cross.

25 **Toucan crossings** are light-controlled crossings which allow cyclists and pedestrians to share crossing space and cross at the same time. They are push-button operated. Pedestrians and cyclists will see the green signal together. Cyclists are permitted to ride across.

Rule 25 *– Toucan crossings can be used by both cyclists and pedestrians*

26 At some crossings there is a bleeping sound or voice signal to indicate to blind or partially sighted people when the steady green figure is showing, and there may be a tactile signal to help deafblind people.

27 **Equestrian crossings** are for horse riders. They have pavement barriers, wider crossing spaces, horse and rider figures in the light panels and either two sets of controls (one higher), or just one higher control panel.

Rule 27 – *Equestrian crossings are used by horse riders. There is often a parallel crossing*

28 **'Staggered' pelican or puffin crossings.** When the crossings on each side of the central refuge are not in line they are two separate crossings. On reaching the central island, press the button again and wait for a steady green figure.

Rule 28 – *Staggered crossings (with an island in the middle) are two separate crossings*

29 **Crossings controlled by an authorised person.** Do not cross the road unless you are signalled to do so by a police officer, traffic warden or school crossing patrol. Always cross in front of them.

30 Where there are no controlled crossing points available it is advisable to cross where there is an island in the middle of the road. Use the Green Cross Code (see Rule 7) to cross to the island and then stop and use it again to cross the second half of the road.

Situations needing extra care

31 **Emergency vehicles.** If an ambulance, fire engine, police or other emergency vehicle approaches using flashing blue lights, headlights and/or sirens, keep off the road.

32 **Buses.** Get on or off a bus only when it has stopped to allow you to do so. Watch out for cyclists when you are getting off. Never cross the road directly behind or in front of a bus. Wait until it has moved off and you can see clearly in both directions.

33 **Tramways.** These may run through pedestrian areas. Their path will be marked out by shallow kerbs, changes in the paving or other road surface, white lines or yellow dots. Cross at designated crossings where provided. Elsewhere treat trams as you would other road vehicles and look both ways along the track before crossing. Do not walk along the track as trams may come up behind you. Trams move quietly and cannot steer to avoid you.

34 **Railway level crossings.** You **MUST NOT** cross or pass a stop line when the red lights show, (including a red pedestrian figure). Also do not cross if an alarm is sounding or the barriers are being lowered. The tone of the alarm may change if another train is approaching. If there are no lights, alarms or barriers, stop, look both ways and listen before crossing. A tactile surface comprising rounded bars running across the direction of pedestrian travel may be installed on the footpath approaching a level crossing to warn visually impaired people of its presence. The tactile surface should extend across the full width of the footway and should be located at an appropriate distance from the barrier or projected line of the barrier.
Law TSRGD, reg 52

35 **Street and pavement repairs.** A pavement may be closed temporarily because it is not safe to use. Take extra care if you are directed to walk in or to cross the road.

Rules for users of powered wheelchairs and powered mobility scooters

(called Invalid Carriages in law)

36 There is one class of manual wheelchair (called a Class 1 invalid carriage) and two classes of powered wheelchairs and powered mobility scooters. Manual wheelchairs and Class 2 vehicles are those with an upper speed limit of 4 mph (6 km/h) and are designed to be used on pavements. Class 3 vehicles are those with an upper speed limit of 8 mph (12 km/h) and are equipped to be used on the road as well as the pavement.

37 When you are on the road you should obey the guidance and rules for other vehicles; when on the pavement you should follow the guidance and rules for pedestrians.

On pavements

38 Pavements are safer than roads and should be used when available. You should give pedestrians priority and show consideration for other pavement users, particularly those with a hearing or visual impairment who may not be aware that you are there.

39 Powered wheelchairs and scooters **MUST NOT** travel faster than 4 mph (6 km/h) on pavements or in pedestrian areas. You may need to reduce your speed to adjust to other pavement users who may not be able to move out of your way quickly enough or where the pavement is too narrow.

Law UICHR 1988 reg 4

40 When moving off the pavement onto the road, you should take special care. Before moving off, always look round and make sure it's safe to join the traffic. Always try to use dropped kerbs when moving off the pavement, even if this means travelling further to locate one. If you have to climb or descend a kerb, always approach it at right angles and don't try to negotiate a kerb higher than the vehicle manufacturer's recommendations.

On the road

41 You should take care when travelling on the road as you may be travelling more slowly than other traffic (your machine is restricted to 8 mph (12 km/h) and may be less visible).

42 When on the road, Class 3 vehicles should travel in the direction of the traffic. Class 2 users should always use the pavement when it is available. When there is no pavement, you should use caution when on the road. Class 2 users should, where possible, travel in the direction of the traffic. If you are travelling at night when lights **MUST** be used, you should travel in the direction of the traffic to avoid confusing other road users.
Law UICHR 1988 reg 9

43 You **MUST** follow the same rules about using lights, indicators and horns as for other road vehicles, if your vehicle is fitted with them. At night, lights **MUST** be used. Be aware that other road users may not see you and you should make yourself more visible – even in the daytime and also at dusk – by, for instance, wearing a reflective jacket or reflective strips on the back of the vehicle.
Law UICHR 1988 reg 9

44 Take extra care at road junctions. When going straight ahead, check to make sure there are no vehicles about to cross your path from the left, the right, or overtaking you and turning left. There are several options for dealing with right turns, especially turning from a major road. If moving into the middle of the road is difficult or dangerous, you can

● stop on the left-hand side of the road and wait for a safe gap in the traffic
● negotiate the turn as a pedestrian, i.e. travel along the pavement and cross the road between pavements where it is safe to do so. Class 3 users should switch the vehicle to the lower speed limit when on pavements.

If the junction is too hazardous, it may be worth considering an alternative route. Similarly, when negotiating major roundabouts (i.e. with two or more lanes) it may be safer for you to use the pavement or find a route which avoids the roundabout altogether.

45 All normal parking restrictions should be observed. Your vehicle should not be left unattended if it causes an obstruction to other pedestrians – especially those in wheelchairs. Parking concessions provided under the Blue Badge scheme (see page 129) will apply to those vehicles displaying a valid badge.

46 These vehicles **MUST NOT** be used on motorways (see Rule 253). They should not be used on unrestricted dual carriageways where the speed limit exceeds 50 mph (80 km/h) but if they are used on these dual carriageways, they **MUST** have a flashing amber beacon. A flashing amber beacon should be used on all other dual carriageways (see Rule 220).

Laws RTRA sect 17(2) & (3), & RVLR reg 17(1) & 26

Horse-drawn vehicles

47 Horse-drawn vehicles used on the highway should be operated and maintained in accordance with standards set out in the Department for Transport's Code of Practice for Horse-Drawn Vehicles. This Code lays down the requirements for a road driving assessment and includes a comprehensive list of safety checks to ensure that a carriage and its fittings are safe and in good working order. The standards set out in the Road Driving Assessment may be required to be met by a Local Authority if an operator wishes to obtain a local authority licence to operate a passenger-carrying service (see page 129).

48 **Safety equipment and clothing.** All horse-drawn vehicles should have two red rear reflectors. It is safer not to drive at night but if you do, a light showing white to the front and red to the rear **MUST** be fitted.
Law RVLR 1989 reg 4

Horse riders

49 **Safety equipment.** Children under the age of 14 **MUST** wear a helmet which complies with the Regulations. It **MUST** be fastened securely. Other riders should also follow these requirements. These requirements do not apply to a child who is a follower of the Sikh religion while wearing a turban.
Laws H(PHYR) Act 1990, sect 1 & H(PHYR) Regulations 1992, reg 3

50 **Other clothing.** You should wear

- boots or shoes with hard soles and heels
- light-coloured or fluorescent clothing in daylight
- reflective clothing if you have to ride at night or in poor visibility.

Rule 50 *– Help yourself to be seen*

51 **At night.** It is safer not to ride on the road at night or in poor visibility, but if you do, make sure you wear reflective clothing and your horse has reflective bands above the fetlock joints. A light which shows white to the front and red to the rear should be fitted, with a band, to the rider's right arm and/or leg/riding boot. If you are leading a horse at night, carry a light in your right hand, showing white to the front and red to the rear, and wear reflective clothing on both you and your horse. It is strongly recommended that a fluorescent/reflective tail guard is also worn by your horse.

Riding

52 Before you take a horse on to a road, you should

- ensure all tack fits well and is in good condition
- make sure you can control the horse.

Always ride with other, less nervous horses if you think that your horse will be nervous of traffic. Never ride a horse without both a saddle and bridle.

53 Before riding off or turning, look behind you to make sure it is safe, then give a clear arm signal.

When riding on the road you should
- keep to the left
- keep both hands on the reins unless you are signalling
- keep both feet in the stirrups
- not carry another person

○ not carry anything which might affect your balance or get tangled up with the reins
○ keep a horse you are leading to your left
○ move in the direction of the traffic flow in a one-way street
○ never ride more than two abreast, and ride in single file on narrow or busy roads and when riding round bends.

54 You **MUST NOT** take a horse onto a footpath or pavement, and you should not take a horse onto a cycle track. Use a bridleway where possible. Equestrian crossings may be provided for horse riders to cross the road and you should use these where available (see page 12). You should dismount at level crossings where a 'horse rider dismount' sign is displayed.
Laws HA 1835 sect 72, R(S)A 1984, sect 129(5)

55 Avoid roundabouts wherever possible. If you use them you should

○ keep to the left and watch out for vehicles crossing your path to leave or join the roundabout
○ signal right when riding across exits to show you are not leaving
○ signal left just before you leave the roundabout.

Other animals

56 **Dogs.** Do not let a dog out on the road on its own. Keep it on a short lead when walking on the pavement, road or path shared with cyclists or horse riders.

57 When in a vehicle make sure dogs or other animals are suitably restrained so they cannot distract you while you are driving or injure you, or themselves, if you stop quickly. A seat belt harness, pet carrier, dog cage or dog guard are ways of restraining animals in cars.

58 **Animals being herded.** These should be kept under control at all times. You should, if possible, send another person along the road in front to warn other road users, especially at a bend or the brow of a hill. It is safer not to move animals after dark, but if you do, then wear reflective clothing and ensure that lights are carried (white at the front and red at the rear of the herd).

Rules for cyclists

These rules are in addition to those in the following sections, which apply to all vehicles (except the motorway section on page 85). See also page 112 – You and your bicycle.

59 **Clothing.** You should wear

- ⋑ a cycle helmet which conforms to current regulations, is the correct size and securely fastened
- ⋑ appropriate clothes for cycling. Avoid clothes which may get tangled in the chain, or in a wheel or may obscure your lights
- ⋑ light-coloured or fluorescent clothing which helps other road users to see you in daylight and poor light
- ⋑ reflective clothing and/or accessories (belt, arm or ankle bands) in the dark.

Rule 59 – *Help yourself to be seen*

60 **At night** your cycle **MUST** have white front and red rear lights lit. It **MUST** also be fitted with a red rear reflector (and amber pedal reflectors, if manufactured after 1/10/85). White front reflectors and spoke reflectors will also help you to be seen. Flashing lights are permitted but it is recommended that cyclists who are riding in areas without street lighting use a steady front lamp.
Law RVLR regs 13, 18 & 24

61 **Cycle Routes and Other Facilities.** Use cycle routes, advanced stop lines, cycle boxes and toucan crossings unless at the time it is unsafe to do so. Use of these facilities is not compulsory and will depend on your experience and skills, but they can make your journey safer.

62 **Cycle Tracks.** These are normally located away from the road, but may occasionally be found alongside footpaths or pavements. Cyclists and pedestrians may be segregated or they may share the same space (unsegregated). When using segregated tracks you **MUST** keep to the side intended for cyclists as the pedestrian side remains a pavement or footpath. Take care when passing pedestrians, especially children, older or disabled people, and allow them plenty of room. Always be prepared to slow down and stop if necessary. Take care near road junctions as you may have difficulty seeing other road users, who might not notice you.
Law HA 1835 sect 72

63 **Cycle Lanes.** These are marked by a white line (which may be broken) along the carriageway (see Rule 140). Keep within the lane when practicable. When leaving a cycle lane check before pulling out that it is safe to do so and signal your intention clearly to other road users. Use of cycle lanes is not compulsory and will depend on your experience and skills, but they can make your journey safer.

64 You **MUST NOT** cycle on a pavement.
Laws HA 1835 sect 72 & R(S)A 1984, sect 129

65 **Bus Lanes.** Most bus lanes may be used by cyclists as indicated on signs. Watch out for people getting on or off a bus. Be very careful when overtaking a bus or leaving a bus lane as you will be entering a busier traffic flow. Do not pass between the kerb and a bus when it is at a stop.

66 **You should**

- keep both hands on the handlebars except when signalling or changing gear
- keep both feet on the pedals
- never ride more than two abreast, and ride in single file on narrow or busy roads and when riding round bends
- not ride close behind another vehicle
- not carry anything which will affect your balance or may get tangled up with your wheels or chain
- be considerate of other road users, particularly blind and partially sighted pedestrians. Let them know you are there when necessary, for example, by ringing your bell if you have one. It is recommended that a bell be fitted.

67 **You should**

- look all around before moving away from the kerb, turning or manoeuvring, to make sure it is safe to do so. Give a clear signal to show other road users what you intend to do (see page 97)
- look well ahead for obstructions in the road, such as drains, pot-holes and parked vehicles so that you do not have to swerve suddenly to avoid them. Leave plenty of room when passing parked vehicles and watch out for doors being opened or pedestrians stepping into your path
- be aware of traffic coming up behind you
- take extra care near road humps, narrowings and other traffic calming features
- take care when overtaking (see Rules 162–169).

68 **You MUST NOT**

- carry a passenger unless your cycle has been built or adapted to carry one
- hold onto a moving vehicle or trailer
- ride in a dangerous, careless or inconsiderate manner
- ride when under the influence of drink or drugs, including medicine.

Law RTA 1988 sects 24, 26, 28, 29 & 30 as amended by RTA 1991

69 You **MUST** obey all traffic signs and traffic light signals.

Laws RTA 1988 sect 36 & TSRGD reg 10(1)

70 When parking your cycle

- ○ find a conspicuous location where it can be seen by passers-by
- ○ use cycle stands or other cycle parking facilities wherever possible
- ○ do not leave it where it would cause an obstruction or hazard to other road users
- ○ secure it well so that it will not fall over and become an obstruction or hazard.

71 You **MUST NOT** cross the stop line when the traffic lights are red. Some junctions have an advanced stop line to enable you to wait and position yourself ahead of other traffic (see Rule 178).

Laws RTA 1988 sect 36 & TSRGD regs 10 & 36(1)

Road junctions

72 **On the left.** When approaching a junction on the left, watch out for vehicles turning in front of you, out of or into the side road. Just before you turn, check for undertaking cyclists or motorcyclists. Do not ride on the inside of vehicles signalling or slowing down to turn left.

73 Pay particular attention to long vehicles which need a lot of room to manoeuvre at corners. Be aware that drivers may not see you. They may have to move over to the right before turning left. Wait until they have completed the manoeuvre because the rear wheels come very close to the kerb while turning. Do not be tempted to ride in the space between them and the kerb.

74 **On the right.** If you are turning right, check the traffic to ensure it is safe, then signal and move to the centre of the road. Wait until there is a safe gap in the oncoming traffic and give a final look before completing the turn. It may be safer to wait on the left until there is a safe gap or to dismount and push your cycle across the road.

75 **Dual carriageways.** Remember that traffic on most dual carriageways moves quickly. When crossing wait for a safe gap and cross each carriageway in turn. Take extra care when crossing slip roads.

Roundabouts

76 Full details about the correct procedure at roundabouts are contained in Rules 184–190. Roundabouts can be hazardous and should be approached with care.

77 You may feel safer walking your cycle round on the pavement or verge. If you decide to ride round keeping to the left-hand lane you should

- ⊃ be aware that drivers may not easily see you
- ⊃ take extra care when cycling across exits. You may need to signal right to show you are not leaving the roundabout
- ⊃ watch out for vehicles crossing your path to leave or join the roundabout.

78 Give plenty of room to long vehicles on the roundabout as they need more space to manoeuvre. Do not ride in the space they need to get round the roundabout. It may be safer to wait until they have cleared the roundabout.

Crossing the road

79 Do not ride across equestrian crossings, as they are for horse riders only. Do not ride across a pelican, puffin or zebra crossing. Dismount and wheel your cycle across.

80 **Toucan crossings.** These are light-controlled crossings which allow cyclists and pedestrians to share crossing space and cross at the same time. They are push-button operated. Pedestrians and cyclists will see the green signal together. Cyclists are permitted to ride across.

81 **Cycle-only crossings.** Cycle tracks on opposite sides of the road may be linked by signalled crossings. You may ride across but you **MUST NOT** cross until the green cycle symbol is showing.
Law TSRGD regs 33(2) & 36(1)

82 **Level crossings/Tramways.** Take extra care when crossing the tracks (see Rule 306). You should dismount at level crossings where a 'cyclist dismount' sign is displayed.

Rules for motorcyclists

These Rules are in addition to those in the following sections which apply to all vehicles. For motorcycle licence requirements see pages 112–114.

General

83 On all journeys, the rider and pillion passenger on a motorcycle, scooter or moped **MUST** wear a protective helmet. This does not apply to a follower of the Sikh religion while wearing a turban. Helmets **MUST** comply with the Regulations and they **MUST** be fastened securely. Riders and passengers of motor tricycles and quadricycles, also called quadbikes, should also wear a protective helmet. Before each journey check that your helmet visor is clean and in good condition.
Laws RTA 1988 sects 16 & 17 & MC(PH)R as amended reg 4

84 It is also advisable to wear eye protectors, which **MUST** comply with the Regulations. Scratched or poorly fitting eye protectors can limit your view when riding, particularly in bright sunshine and the hours of darkness. Consider wearing ear protection. Strong boots, gloves and suitable clothing may help to protect you if you are involved in a collision.
Laws RTA sect 18 & MC(EP)R as amended reg 4

85 You **MUST NOT** carry more than one pillion passenger who **MUST** sit astride the machine on a proper seat. They should face forward with both feet on the footrests. You **MUST NOT** carry a pillion passenger unless your motor cycle is designed to do so. Provisional licence holders **MUST NOT** carry a pillion passenger.
Laws RTA 1988 sect 23, MV(DL)R 1999 reg 16(6) & CUR 1986 reg 102

86 **Daylight riding.** Make yourself as visible as possible from the side as well as the front and rear. You could wear a light or brightly coloured helmet and fluorescent clothing or strips. Dipped headlights, even in good daylight, may also make you more conspicuous. However, be aware that other vehicle drivers may still not have seen you, or judged your distance or speed correctly, especially at junctions.

Rule 86 – Help yourself to be seen

87 **Riding in the dark.** Wear reflective clothing or strips to improve your visibility in the dark. These reflect light from the headlamps of other vehicles, making you visible from a longer distance. See Rules113–116 for lighting requirements.

88 **Manoeuvring.** You should be aware of what is behind and to the sides before manoeuvring. Look behind you; use mirrors if they are fitted. When in traffic queues look out for pedestrians crossing between vehicles and vehicles emerging from junctions or changing lanes. Position yourself so that drivers in front can see you in their mirrors. Additionally, when filtering in slow-moving traffic, take care and keep your speed low.

Remember:
Observation – Signal – Manoeuvre.

Rules for drivers and motorcyclists

89 **Vehicle condition.** You **MUST** ensure your vehicle and trailer comply with the full requirements of the Road Vehicles (Construction and Use) Regulations and Road Vehicles Lighting Regulations (see page 118).

Fitness to drive

90 Make sure that you are fit to drive. You **MUST** report to the Driver and Vehicle Licensing Agency (DVLA) any health condition likely to affect your driving.
Law RTA 1988 sect 94

91 Driving when you are tired greatly increases your risk of collision. To minimise this risk

- ➲ make sure you are fit to drive. Do not begin a journey if you are tired. Get a good night's sleep before embarking on a long journey
- ➲ avoid undertaking long journeys between midnight and 6 am, when natural alertness is at a minimum
- ➲ plan your journey to take sufficient breaks. A minimum break of at least 15 minutes after every two hours of driving is recommended
- ➲ if you feel at all sleepy, stop in a safe place. Do not stop on the hard shoulder of a motorway
- ➲ the most effective ways to counter sleepiness are to drink, for example, two cups of caffeinated coffee and to take a short nap (at least 15 minutes).

92 **Vision.** You **MUST** be able to read a vehicle number plate, in good daylight, from a distance of 20 metres (or 20.5 metres where the old style number plate is used). If you need to wear glasses (or contact lenses) to do this, you **MUST** wear them at all times while driving. The police have the power to require a driver to undertake an eyesight test.
Laws RTA 1988 sect 96 & MV(DL)R reg 40 & sch 8

93 Slow down, and if necessary stop, if you are dazzled by bright sunlight.

94 At night or in poor visibility, do not use tinted glasses, lenses or visors if they restrict your vision.

Alcohol and drugs

95

Do not drink and drive as it will seriously affect your judgement and abilities. You **MUST NOT** drive with a breath alcohol level higher than 35 microgrammes/100 millilitres of breath or a blood alcohol level of more than 80 milligrammes/100 millilitres of blood. Alcohol will

- give a false sense of confidence
- reduce co-ordination and slow down reactions
- affect judgement of speed, distance and risk
- reduce your driving ability, even if you're below the legal limit
- take time to leave your body; you may be unfit to drive in the evening after drinking at lunchtime, or in the morning after drinking the previous evening.

The best solution is not to drink at all when planning to drive because any amount of alcohol affects your ability to drive safely. If you are going to drink, arrange another means of transport.

Law RTA 1988 sects 4, 5 & 11(2)

96

You **MUST NOT** drive under the influence of drugs or medicine. Check the instructions or ask your doctor or pharmacist. Using illegal drugs is highly dangerous. Never take them if you intend to drive; the effects are unpredictable, but can be even more severe than alcohol and may result in fatal or serious road crashes.

Law RTA 1988 sect 4

97

Before setting off. You should ensure that

- you have planned your route and allowed sufficient time
- clothing and footwear do not prevent you using the controls in the correct manner
- you know where all the controls are and how to use them before you need them. Not all vehicles are the same; do not wait until it is too late to find out
- your mirrors and seat are adjusted correctly to ensure comfort, full control and maximum vision
- head restraints are properly adjusted to reduce the risk of neck and spine injuries in the event of a collision
- you have sufficient fuel before commencing your journey, especially if it includes motorway driving. It can be dangerous to lose power when driving in traffic
- ensure your vehicle is legal and roadworthy
- switch off your mobile phone.

Rule 97 – *Make sure head restraints are properly adjusted*

98 **Vehicle towing and loading.** As a driver

◯ you **MUST NOT** tow more than your licence permits. If you passed a car test after 1 Jan 1997 you are restricted on the weight of trailer you can tow

◯ you **MUST NOT** overload your vehicle or trailer. You should not tow a weight greater than that recommended by the manufacturer of your vehicle

◯ you **MUST** secure your load and it **MUST NOT** stick out dangerously. Make sure any heavy or sharp objects and any animals are secured safely. If there is a collision, they might hit someone inside the vehicle and cause serious injury

◯ you should properly distribute the weight in your caravan or trailer with heavy items mainly over the axle(s) and ensure a downward load on the tow ball. Manufacturer's recommended weight and tow ball load should not be exceeded. This should avoid the possibility of swerving or snaking and going out of control. If this does happen, ease off the accelerator and reduce speed gently to regain control

◯ carrying a load or pulling a trailer may require you to adjust the headlights.

In the event of a breakdown, be aware that towing a vehicle on a tow rope is potentially dangerous. You should consider professional recovery.

Laws CUR reg 100 & MV(DL)R reg 43

Seat belts and child restraints

99

You **MUST** wear a seat belt in cars, vans and other goods vehicles if one is fitted (see table below). Adults, and children aged 14 years and over, **MUST** use a seat belt or child restraint, where fitted, when seated in minibuses, buses and coaches. Exemptions are allowed for the holders of medical exemption certificates and those making deliveries or collections in goods vehicles when travelling less than 50 metres (approx 162 feet).

Laws RTA 1988 sects 14 & 15, MV(WSB)R, MV(WSBCFS)R & MV(WSB)(A)R

Seat belt requirements. This table summarises the main legal requirements for wearing seat belts in cars, vans and other goods vehicles

	Front seat	Rear seat	Who is responsible?
Driver	Seat belt **MUST** be worn if fitted		**Driver**
Child under 3 years of age	Correct child restraint **MUST** be used	Correct child restraint **MUST** be used. If one is not available in a taxi, may travel unrestrained.	**Driver**
Child from 3rd birthday up to 1.35 metres in height (or 12th birthday, whichever they reach first)	Correct child restraint **MUST** be used	Correct child restraint **MUST** be used where seat belts fitted. **MUST** use adult belt if correct child restraint is not available in a licensed taxi or private hire vehicle, or for reasons of unexpected necessity over a short distance, or if two occupied restraints prevent fitment of a third.	**Driver**
Child over 1.35 metres (approx 4ft 5ins) in height or 12 or 13 years	Adult seat belt **MUST** be worn if available	Adult seat belt **MUST** be worn if available	**Driver**
Adult passengers aged 14 and over	Seat belt **MUST** be worn if available	Seat belt **MUST** be worn if available	**Passenger**

Rule 100 – *Make sure that a child uses a suitable restraint which is correctly adjusted*

100 The driver **MUST** ensure that all children under 14 years of age in cars, vans and other goods vehicles wear seat belts or sit in an approved child restraint where required (see table above). If a child is under 1.35 metres (approx 4 feet 5 inches) tall, a baby seat, child seat, booster seat or booster cushion **MUST** be used suitable for the child's weight and fitted to the manufacturer's instructions.
Laws RTA 1988 sects 14 & 15, MV(WSB)R, MV(WSBCFS)R & MV(WSB)(A)R

101 A rear-facing baby seat **MUST NOT** be fitted into a seat protected by an active frontal airbag, as in a crash it can cause serious injury or death to the child.
Laws RTA 1988 sects 14 & 15, MV(WSB)R, MV(WSBCFS)R & MV(WSB)(A)R

102 **Children in cars, vans and other goods vehicles.** Drivers who are carrying children in cars, vans and other goods vehicles should also ensure that

- children should get into the vehicle through the door nearest the kerb
- child restraints are properly fitted to manufacturer's instructions
- children do not sit behind the rear seats in an estate car or hatchback, unless a special child seat has been fitted
- the child safety door locks, where fitted, are used when children are in the vehicle
- children are kept under control.

This section should be read by all drivers, motorcyclists, cyclists and horse riders. The rules in *The Highway Code* do not give you the right of way in any circumstance, but they advise you when you should give way to others. Always give way if it can help to avoid an incident.

Signals

103 Signals warn and inform other road users, including pedestrians (see page 97), of your intended actions. You should always

- give clear signals in plenty of time, having checked it is not misleading to signal at that time
- use them to advise other road users before changing course or direction, stopping or moving off
- cancel them after use
- make sure your signals will not confuse others. If, for instance, you want to stop after a side road, do not signal until you are passing the road. If you signal earlier it may give the impression that you intend to turn into the road. Your brake lights will warn traffic behind you that you are slowing down
- use an arm signal to emphasise or reinforce your signal if necessary. Remember that signalling does not give you priority.

104 You should also
- watch out for signals given by other road users and proceed only when you are satisfied that it is safe
- be aware that an indicator on another vehicle may not have been cancelled.

105 You **MUST** obey signals given by police officers, traffic officers, traffic wardens (see pages 104-105) and signs used by school crossing patrols.

Laws RTRA sect 28, RTA 1988 sect 35, TMA 2004 sect 6, & FTWO art 3

Police stopping procedures. If the police want to stop your vehicle they will, where possible, attract your attention by

- flashing blue lights, headlights or sounding their siren or horn, usually from behind
- directing you to pull over to the side by pointing and/or using the left indicator.

You **MUST** then pull over and stop as soon as it is safe to do so. Then switch off your engine.
Law RTA 1988 sect 163

Other stopping procedures
Vehicle & Operator Services Agency Officers have powers to stop vehicles on all roads, including motorways and trunk roads, in England and Wales. They will attract your attention by flashing amber lights

- either from the front requesting you to follow them to a safe place to stop
- or from behind directing you to pull over to the side by pointing and/or using the left indicator.

It is an offence not to comply with their directions. You **MUST** obey any signals given (see page 99).
Laws RTA 1988, sect 67, & PRA 2002, sect 41 & sched 5(8)

Highways Agency Traffic Officers have powers to stop vehicles on most motorways and some 'A' class roads, in England only. If HA traffic officers in uniform want to stop your vehicle on safety grounds (e.g. an insecure load) they will, where possible, attract your attention by

- flashing amber lights, usually from behind
- directing you to pull over to the side by pointing and/or using the left indicator.

You **MUST** then pull over and stop as soon as it is safe to do so. Then switch off your engine. It is an offence not to comply with their directions (see page 99).
Law RTA1988, sects 35 &163 as amended by TMA 2004, sect 6

109 **Traffic light signals and traffic signs.** You **MUST** obey all traffic light signals (see page 96) and traffic signs giving orders, including temporary signals & signs (see pages 100–107). Make sure you know, understand and act on all other traffic and information signs and road markings (see pages 100–111).

Laws RTA 1988 sect 36 & TSRGD regs 10, 15, 16, 25, 26, 27, 28, 29, 36, 38 & 40

110 **Flashing headlights.** Only flash your headlights to let other road users know that you are there. Do not flash your headlights to convey any other message or intimidate other road users.

 111 Never assume that flashing headlights is a signal inviting you to proceed. Use your own judgement and proceed carefully.

 112 **The horn.** Use only while your vehicle is moving and you need to warn other road users of your presence. Never sound your horn aggressively. You **MUST NOT** use your horn

- while stationary on the road
- when driving in a built-up area between the hours of 11.30 pm and 7.00 am

except when another road user poses a danger.

Law CUR reg 99

Lighting requirements

113 **You MUST**

- ensure all sidelights and rear registration plate lights are lit between sunset and sunrise
- use headlights at night, except on a road which has lit street lighting. These roads are generally restricted to a speed limit of 30 mph (48 km/h) unless otherwise specified
- use headlights when visibility is seriously reduced (see Rule 226).

Night (the hours of darkness) is defined as the period between half an hour after sunset and half an hour before sunrise.

Laws RVLR regs 3, 24, & 25, (In Scotland – RTRA 1984 sect 82 (as amended by NRSWA, para 59 of sched 8))

114 **You MUST NOT**

- ○ use any lights in a way which would dazzle or cause discomfort to other road users, including pedestrians, cyclists and horse riders
- ○ use front or rear fog lights unless visibility is seriously reduced. You **MUST** switch them off when visibility improves to avoid dazzling other road users (see Rule 226).

In stationary queues of traffic, drivers should apply the parking brake and, once the following traffic has stopped, take their foot off the footbrake to deactivate the vehicle brake lights. This will minimise glare to road users behind until the traffic moves again.

Law RVLR reg 27

115 **You should also**

- ○ use dipped headlights, or dim-dip if fitted, at night in built-up areas and in dull daytime weather, to ensure that you can be seen
- ○ keep your headlights dipped when overtaking until you are level with the other vehicle and then change to main beam if necessary, unless this would dazzle oncoming road users
- ○ slow down, and if necessary stop, if you are dazzled by oncoming headlights.

116 **Hazard warning lights.** These may be used when your vehicle is stationary, to warn that it is temporarily obstructing traffic. Never use them as an excuse for dangerous or illegal parking. You **MUST NOT** use hazard warning lights while driving or being towed unless you are on a motorway or unrestricted dual carriageway and you need to warn drivers behind you of a hazard or obstruction ahead. Only use them for long enough to ensure that your warning has been observed.

Law RVLR reg 27

Control of the vehicle

Braking

117 **In normal circumstances.** The safest way to brake is to do so early and lightly. Brake more firmly as you begin to stop. Ease the pressure off just before the vehicle comes to rest to avoid a jerky stop.

In an emergency. Brake immediately. Try to avoid braking so harshly that you lock your wheels. Locked wheels can lead to loss of control.

119 **Skids.** Skidding is usually caused by the driver braking, accelerating or steering too harshly or driving too fast for the road conditions. If skidding occurs, remove the cause by releasing the brake pedal fully or easing off the accelerator. Turn the steering wheel in the direction of the skid. For example, if the rear of the vehicle skids to the right, steer immediately to the right to recover.

Rule 119 – *Rear of the car skids to the right. Driver steers to the right*

120 **ABS.** If your vehicle is fitted with anti-lock brakes, you should follow the advice given in the vehicle handbook. However, in the case of an emergency, apply the footbrake firmly; do not release the pressure until the vehicle has slowed to the desired speed. The ABS should ensure that steering control will be retained, but do not assume that a vehicle with ABS will stop in a shorter distance.

121 **Brakes affected by water.** If you have driven through deep water your brakes may be less effective. Test them at the first safe opportunity by pushing gently on the brake pedal to make sure that they work. If they are not fully effective, gently apply light pressure while driving slowly. This will help to dry them out.

122 **Coasting.** This term describes a vehicle travelling in neutral or with the clutch pressed down. It can reduce driver control because

- ➲ engine braking is eliminated
- ➲ vehicle speed downhill will increase quickly
- ➲ increased use of the footbrake can reduce its effectiveness
- ➲ steering response will be affected, particularly on bends and corners
- ➲ it may be more difficult to select the appropriate gear when needed.

123 **The Driver and the Environment.** You **MUST NOT** leave a parked vehicle unattended with the engine running or leave a vehicle engine running unnecessarily while that vehicle is stationary on a public road. Generally, if the vehicle is stationary and is likely to remain so for more than a couple of minutes, you should apply the parking brake and switch off the engine to reduce emissions and noise pollution. However it is permissible to leave the engine running if the vehicle is stationary in traffic or for diagnosing faults.

Law CUR regs 98 & 107

Speed Limits

Type of vehicle	Built-up areas* mph (km/h)	Single carriageways mph (km/h)	Double carriageways mph (km/h)	Motorways mph (km/h)
Cars & motorcycles (including car-derived vans up to 2 tonnes maximum laden weight)	30 (48)	60 (96)	70 (112)	70 (112)
Cars towing caravans or trailers (including car-derived vans and motorcycles)	30 (48)	50 (80)	60 (96)	60 (96)
Buses, coaches and minibuses (not exceeding 12 metres in overall length)	30 (48)	50 (80)	60 (96)	70** (112)
Goods vehicles (not exceeding 7.5 tonnes maximum laden weight)	30 (48)	50 (80)	60 (96)	70 (112)
Goods vehicles (exceeding 7.5 tonnes maximum laden weight)	30 (48)	40 (64)	50 (80)	60 (96)

* *The 30 mph limit usually applies to all traffic on all roads with street lighting unless signs show otherwise.*
** *60 mph (96 km/h) if articulated or towing a trailer.*

Speed limits

124 You **MUST NOT** exceed the maximum speed limits for the road and for your vehicle (see the table on page 37). The presence of street lights generally means that there is a 30 mph (48 km/h) speed limit unless otherwise specified.

Law RTRA sects 81, 86, 89 & sch 6

125 The speed limit is the absolute maximum and does not mean it is safe to drive at that speed irrespective of conditions. Driving at speeds too fast for the road and traffic conditions is dangerous. You should always reduce your speed when

- the road layout or condition presents hazards, such as bends
- sharing the road with pedestrians, cyclists and horse riders, particularly children, and motorcyclists
- weather conditions make it safer to do so
- driving at night as it is more difficult to see other road users.

126 **Stopping Distances.** Drive at a speed that will allow you to stop well within the distance you can see to be clear. You should

Typical Stopping Distances

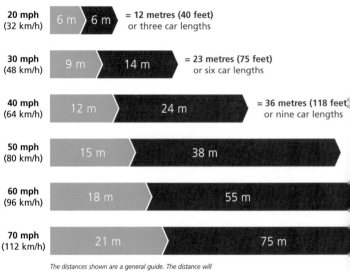

Speed	Thinking distance	Braking distance	Total
20 mph (32 km/h)	6 m	6 m	= 12 metres (40 feet) or three car lengths
30 mph (48 km/h)	9 m	14 m	= 23 metres (75 feet) or six car lengths
40 mph (64 km/h)	12 m	24 m	= 36 metres (118 feet) or nine car lengths
50 mph (80 km/h)	15 m	38 m	
60 mph (96 km/h)	18 m	55 m	
70 mph (112 km/h)	21 m	75 m	

The distances shown are a general guide. The distance will depend on your attention (thinking distance), the road surface, the weather conditions and the condition of your vehicle at the time.

Rule 126 – *Use a fixed point to help measure a two-second gap*

↻ leave enough space between you and the vehicle
in front so that you can pull up safely if it suddenly
slows down or stops. The safe rule is never to get
closer than the overall stopping distance (see Typical
Stopping Distances diagram, shown below)

↻ allow at least a two-second gap between you and
the vehicle in front on roads carrying faster-moving
traffic and in tunnels where visibility is reduced. The
gap should be at least doubled on wet roads and
increased still further on icy roads

↻ remember, large vehicles and motorcycles need a
greater distance to stop. If driving a large vehicle
in a tunnel, you should allow a four-second gap
between you and the vehicle in front.

If you have to stop in a tunnel, leave at least a 5-metre
gap between you and the vehicle in front.

Thinking Distance	Braking Distance

Average car length = 4 metres (13 feet)

= **53 metres (175 feet)**
or thirteen car lengths

= **73 metres (240 feet)**
or eighteen car lengths

= **96 metres (315 feet)**
or twenty-four car lengths

Lines and lane markings on the road

Diagrams of all lines are on pages 108–111.

127 **A broken white line.** This marks the centre of the road. When this line lengthens and the gaps shorten, it means that there is a hazard ahead. Do not cross it unless you can see the road is clear and wish to overtake or turn off.

128 **Double white lines where the line nearest to you is broken.** This means you may cross the lines to overtake if it is safe, provided you can complete the manoeuvre before reaching a solid white line on your side. White direction arrows on the road indicate that you need to get back onto your side of the road.

129 **Double white lines where the line nearest you is solid.** This means you **MUST NOT** cross or straddle it unless it is safe and you need to enter adjoining premises or a side road. You may cross the line if necessary, provided the road is clear, to pass a stationary vehicle, or overtake a pedal cycle, horse or road maintenance vehicle, if they are travelling at 10 mph (16 km/h) or less.

Laws RTA 1988 sect 36 & TSRGD regs 10 & 26

130 **Areas of white diagonal stripes** or chevrons painted on the road. These are to separate traffic lanes or to protect traffic turning right.

◐ If the area is bordered by a broken white line, you should not enter the area unless it is necessary and you can see that it is safe to do so.

◐ If the area is marked with chevrons and bordered by solid white lines you **MUST NOT** enter it except in an emergency.

Laws MT(E&W)R regs 5, 9, 10 & 16, MT(S)R regs 4, 8, 9 & 14, RTA sect 36 & TSRGD 10(1)

131 **Lane dividers.** These are short, broken white lines which are used on wide carriageways to divide them into lanes. You should keep between them.

Rule 132 *– Reflective road studs mark the lanes and edges of the carriageway*

132 **Reflective road studs** may be used with white lines.

- ➲ White studs mark the lanes or the middle of the road.
- ➲ Red studs mark the left edge of the road.
- ➲ Amber studs mark the central reservation of a dual carriageway or motorway.
- ➲ Green studs mark the edge of the main carriageway at lay-bys and slip roads.
- ➲ Green/yellow studs indicate temporary adjustments to lane layouts, e.g. where road works are taking place.

Multi-lane carriageways

133 ### Lane discipline
If you need to change lane, first use your mirrors and if necessary take a quick sideways glance to make sure you will not force another road user to change course or speed. When it is safe to do so, signal to indicate your intentions to other road users and when clear, move over.

134 You should follow the signs and road markings and get into the lane as directed. In congested road conditions do not change lanes unnecessarily. Merging in turn is recommended but only if safe and appropriate when vehicles are travelling at a very low speed, e.g. when approaching road works or a road traffic incident. It is not recommended at high speed.

Single carriageway

135 Where a single carriageway has three lanes and the road markings or signs do not give priority to traffic in either direction

- ◯ use the middle lane only for overtaking or turning right. Remember, you have no more right to use the middle lane than a driver coming from the opposite direction
- ◯ do not use the right-hand lane.

136 Where a single carriageway has four or more lanes, use only the lanes that signs or markings indicate.

Dual carriageways

A dual carriageway is a road which has a central reservation to separate the carriageways.

137 On a two-lane dual carriageway you should stay in the left-hand lane. Use the right-hand lane for overtaking or turning right. After overtaking, move back to the left-hand lane when it is safe to do so.

138 On a three-lane dual carriageway, you may use the middle lane or the right-hand lane to overtake but return to the middle and then the left-hand lane when it is safe.

139 **Climbing and crawler lanes.** These are provided on some hills. Use this lane if you are driving a slow-moving vehicle or if there are vehicles behind you wishing to overtake. Be aware of the signs and road markings which indicate the lane is about to end.

140 **Cycle lanes.** These are shown by road markings and signs. You **MUST NOT** drive or park in a cycle lane marked by a solid white line during its times of operation. Do not drive or park in a cycle lane marked by a broken white line unless it is unavoidable. You **MUST NOT** park in any cycle lane whilst waiting restrictions apply.
Law RTRA sects 5 & 8

141 **Bus lanes.** These are shown by road markings and signs that indicate which (if any) other vehicles are permitted to use the bus lane. Unless otherwise indicated, you should not drive in a bus lane during its period of operation. You may enter a bus lane to stop, to load or unload where this is not prohibited.

142 **High-occupancy vehicle lanes and other designated vehicle lanes.** Lanes may be restricted for use by particular types of vehicle; these restrictions may apply some or all of the time. The operating times and vehicle types will be indicated on the accompanying traffic signs. You **MUST NOT** drive in such lanes during their times of operation unless signs indicate that your vehicle is permitted (see page 106).

Vehicles permitted to use designated lanes may or may not include cycles, buses, taxis, licensed private hire vehicles, motorcycles, heavy goods vehicles (HGVs) and high-occupancy vehicles (HOVs).

Where HOV lanes are in operation, they **MUST ONLY** be used by

- ● vehicles containing at least the minimum number of people indicated on the traffic signs
- ● any other vehicles, such as buses and motorcycles, as indicated on signs prior to the start of the lane, irrespective of the number of occupants.

Laws RTRA sects 5 & 8, & RTA 1988, sect 36

143 **One-way streets.** Traffic **MUST** travel in the direction indicated by signs. Buses and/or cycles may have a contraflow lane. Choose the correct lane for your exit as soon as you can. Do not change lanes suddenly. Unless road signs or markings indicate otherwise, you should use

- ● the left-hand lane when going left
- ● the right-hand lane when going right
- ● the most appropriate lane when going straight ahead. Remember – traffic could be passing on both sides.

Laws RTA 1988 sect 36 & RTRA sects 5 & 8

General advice

144 **You MUST NOT**

- ● drive dangerously
- ● drive without due care and attention
- ● drive without reasonable consideration for other road users.

Law RTA 1988 sects 2 & 3 as amended by RTA 1991

You **MUST NOT** drive on or over a pavement, footpath or bridleway except to gain lawful access to property, or in the case of an emergency.
Laws HA 1835 sect 72 & RTA 1988 sect 34

 Adapt your driving to the appropriate type and condition of road you are on. In particular

- ⮑ do not treat speed limits as a target. It is often not appropriate or safe to drive at the maximum speed limit
- ⮑ take the road and traffic conditions into account. Be prepared for unexpected or difficult situations, for example, the road being blocked beyond a blind bend. Be prepared to adjust your speed as a precaution
- ⮑ where there are junctions, be prepared for road users emerging
- ⮑ in side roads and country lanes look out for unmarked junctions where nobody has priority
- ⮑ be prepared to stop at traffic control systems, road works, pedestrian crossings or traffic lights as necessary
- ⮑ try to anticipate what pedestrians and cyclists might do. If pedestrians, particularly children, are looking the other way, they may step out into the road without seeing you.

147 **Be considerate.** Be careful of and considerate towards all types of road users, especially those requiring extra care (see Rule 204). You should

- ⮑ try to be understanding if other road users cause problems; they may be inexperienced or not know the area well
- ⮑ be patient; remember that anyone can make a mistake
- ⮑ not allow yourself to become agitated or involved if someone is behaving badly on the road. This will only make the situation worse. Pull over, calm down and, when you feel relaxed, continue your journey
- ⮑ slow down and hold back if a road user pulls out into your path at a junction. Allow them to get clear. Do not over-react by driving too close behind to intimidate them
- ⮑ do not throw anything out of a vehicle, for example, cigarette ends, cans, paper or carrier bags. This can endanger other road users, particularly motorcyclists and cyclists.

148 **Safe driving and riding needs concentration.**
Avoid distractions when driving or riding such as

- loud music (this may mask other sounds)
- trying to read maps
- inserting a cassette or CD or tuning a radio
- arguing with your passengers or other
  road users
- eating and drinking
- smoking

You **MUST NOT** smoke in public transport
vehicles or in vehicles used for work purposes
in certain prescribed circumstances. Separate
regulations apply to England, Wales and Scotland.
Laws TSf(EV) regs 2007, TSfP(W) regs 2007 & TPSCP(S) regs 2006

Mobile phones and in-vehicle technology

149 You **MUST** exercise proper control of your vehicle
at all times. You **MUST NOT** use a hand-held
mobile phone, or similar device, when driving or
when supervising a learner driver, except to call
999 or 112 in a genuine emergency when it is
unsafe or impractical to stop. Never use a hand-
held microphone when driving. Using hands-free
equipment is also likely to distract your attention
from the road. It is far safer not to use any
telephone while you are driving or riding – find a
safe place to stop first or use the voicemail facility
and listen to messages later.
Laws RTA 1988 sects 2 & 3 & CUR regs 104 & 110

150 There is a danger of driver distraction being
caused by in-vehicle systems such as satellite
navigation systems, congestion warning systems,
PCs, multi-media, etc. You **MUST** exercise
proper control of your vehicle at all times. Do
not rely on driver assistance systems such as
cruise control or lane departure warnings. They
are available to assist but you should not reduce
your concentration levels. Do not be distracted
by maps or screen-based information (such as
navigation or vehicle management systems)
while driving or riding. If necessary find
a safe place to stop.
Laws RTA 1988 sects 2 & 3 & CUR reg 104

Rule 151 – Do not block access to a side road

151 **In slow-moving traffic.** You should

- reduce the distance between you and the vehicle ahead to maintain traffic flow
- never get so close to the vehicle in front that you cannot stop safely
- leave enough space to be able to manoeuvre if the vehicle in front breaks down or an emergency vehicle needs to get past
- not change lanes to the left to overtake
- allow access into and from side roads, as blocking these will add to congestion
- be aware of cyclists and motorcyclists who may be passing on either side.

152 **Driving in built-up areas**
Residential streets. You should drive slowly and carefully on streets where there are likely to be pedestrians, cyclists and parked cars. In some areas a 20 mph (32 km/h) maximum speed limit may be in force. Look out for

- vehicles emerging from junctions or driveways
- vehicles moving off
- car doors opening
- pedestrians
- children running out from between parked cars
- cyclists and motorcyclists.

Rule 153 – Chicanes may be used to slow traffic down

153 **Traffic-calming measures.** On some roads there are features such as road humps, chicanes and narrowings which are intended to slow you down. When you approach these features reduce your speed. Allow cyclists and motorcyclists room to pass through them. Maintain a reduced speed along the whole of the stretch of road within the calming measures. Give way to oncoming road users if directed to do so by signs. You should not overtake other moving road users while in these areas.

Country roads

154 Take extra care on country roads and reduce your speed at approaches to bends, which can be sharper than they appear, and at junctions and turnings, which may be partially hidden. Be prepared for pedestrians, horse riders, cyclists, slow-moving farm vehicles or mud on the road surface. Make sure you can stop within the distance you can see to be clear. You should also reduce your speed where country roads enter villages.

155 **Single-track roads.** These are only wide enough for one vehicle. They may have special passing places. If you see a vehicle coming towards you, or the driver behind wants to overtake, pull into a passing place on your left, or wait opposite a passing place on your right. Give way to vehicles coming uphill whenever you can. If necessary, reverse until you reach a passing place to let the other vehicle pass. Slow down when passing pedestrians, cyclists and horse riders.

156 Do not park in passing places.

Vehicles prohibited from using roads and pavements

157 Certain motorised vehicles do not meet the construction and technical requirements for road vehicles and are generally not intended, not suitable and not legal for road, pavement, footpath, cycle path or bridleway use. These include most types of miniature motorcycles, also called mini motos, and motorised scooters, also called go peds, which are powered by electric or internal combustion engines. These types of vehicle **MUST NOT** be used on roads, pavements, footpaths or bridleways.

Laws RTA 1988 sects 34, 41a, 42, 47, 63 & 66, HA 1835, sect 72, & R(S)A sect 129

158 Certain models of motorcycles, motor tricycles and quadricycles, also called quad bikes, are suitable only for off-road use and do not meet legal standards for use on roads. Vehicles that do not meet these standards **MUST NOT** be used on roads. They **MUST NOT** be used on pavements, footpaths, cycle paths or bridleways either. You **MUST** make sure that any motorcycle, motor tricycle, quadricycle or any other motor vehicle meets legal standards and is properly registered, taxed and insured before using it on the roads. Even when registered, taxed and insured for the road, vehicles **MUST NOT** be used on pavements.

Laws RTA 1988 sects 34, 41a, 42, 47, 63, 66 & 156, HA 1835, sect 72, R(S)A sect 129, & VERA sects 1, 29, 31A, & 43A

General rules

159

Before moving off you should

- ⟴ use all mirrors to check the road is clear
- ⟴ look round to check the blind spots (the areas you are unable to see in the mirrors)
- ⟴ signal if necessary before moving out
- ⟴ look round for a final check.

Move off only when it is safe to do so.

Rule 159 – *Check the blind spot before moving off*

160

Once moving you should

- ⟴ keep to the left, unless road signs or markings indicate otherwise. The exceptions are when you want to overtake, turn right or pass parked vehicles or pedestrians in the road
- ⟴ keep well to the left on right-hand bends. This will improve your view of the road and help avoid the risk of colliding with traffic approaching from the opposite direction
- ⟴ drive with both hands on the wheel where possible. This will help you to remain in full control of the vehicle at all times

- be aware of other road users, especially cycles and motorcycles who may be filtering through the traffic. These are more difficult to see than larger vehicles and their riders are particularly vulnerable. Give them plenty of room, especially if you are driving a long vehicle or towing a trailer
- select a lower gear before you reach a long downhill slope. This will help to control your speed
- when towing, remember the extra length will affect overtaking and manoeuvring. The extra weight will also affect the braking and acceleration.

161 **Mirrors.** All mirrors should be used effectively throughout your journey. You should

- use your mirrors frequently so that you always know what is behind and to each side of you
- use them in good time before you signal or change direction or speed
- be aware that mirrors do not cover all areas and there will be blind spots. You will need to look round and check.

Remember: Mirrors – Signal – Manoeuvre

Overtaking

Before overtaking you should make sure

- the road is sufficiently clear ahead
- road users are not beginning to overtake you
- there is a suitable gap in front of the road user you plan to overtake.

Overtake only when it is safe and legal to do so. You should

- not get too close to the vehicle you intend to overtake
- use your mirrors, signal when it is safe to do so, take a quick sideways glance if necessary into the blind spot area and then start to move out
- not assume that you can simply follow a vehicle ahead which is overtaking; there may only be enough room for one vehicle

- move quickly past the vehicle you are overtaking, once you have started to overtake. Allow plenty of room. Move back to the left as soon as you can but do not cut in
- take extra care at night and in poor visibility when it is harder to judge speed and distance
- give way to oncoming vehicles before passing parked vehicles or other obstructions on your side of the road
- only overtake on the left if the vehicle in front is signalling to turn right, and there is room to do so
- stay in your lane if traffic is moving slowly in queues. If the queue on your right is moving more slowly than you are, you may pass on the left
- give motorcyclists, cyclists and horse riders at least as much room as you would when overtaking a car (see Rules 211–215).

Remember: Mirrors – Signal – Manoeuvre

Rule 163 – *Give vulnerable road users at least as much space as you would a car*

164 **Large vehicles.** Overtaking these is more difficult. You should

- ⊖ drop back. This will increase your ability to see ahead and should allow the driver of the large vehicle to see you in their mirrors. Getting too close to large vehicles, including agricultural vehicles such as a tractor with a trailer or other fixed equipment, will obscure your view of the road ahead and there may be another slow-moving vehicle in front

- ⊖ make sure that you have enough room to complete your overtaking manoeuvre before committing yourself. It takes longer to pass a large vehicle. If in doubt do not overtake

- ⊖ not assume you can follow a vehicle ahead which is overtaking a long vehicle. If a problem develops, they may abort overtaking and pull back in.

Rule 164 – Do not cut in too quickly

165 You **MUST NOT** overtake

- ⊖ if you would have to cross or straddle double white lines with a solid line nearest to you (but see Rule129)

- ⊖ if you would have to enter an area designed to divide traffic, if it is surrounded by a solid white line

- ⊖ the nearest vehicle to a pedestrian crossing, especially when it has stopped to let pedestrians cross

- ⊖ if you would have to enter a lane reserved for buses, trams or cycles during its hours of operation

- ⊖ after a 'No Overtaking' sign and until you pass a sign cancelling the restriction.

Laws RTA 1988 sect 36, TSRGD regs 10, 22, 23 & 24, ZPPPCRGD reg 24

166 **DO NOT** overtake if there is any doubt, or where you cannot see far enough ahead to be sure it is safe. For example, when you are approaching

- a corner or bend
- a hump bridge
- the brow of a hill.

167 **DO NOT** overtake where you might come into conflict with other road users. For example

- approaching or at a road junction on either side of the road
- where the road narrows
- when approaching a school crossing patrol
- between the kerb and a bus or tram when it is at a stop
- where traffic is queuing at junctions or road works
- when you would force another road user to swerve or slow down
- at a level crossing
- when a road user is indicating right, even if you believe the signal should have been cancelled. Do not take a risk; wait for the signal to be cancelled
- stay behind if you are following a cyclist approaching a roundabout or junction, and you intend to turn left
- when a tram is standing at a kerbside tram stop and there is no clearly marked passing lane for other traffic.

168 **Being overtaken.** If a driver is trying to overtake you, maintain a steady course and speed, slowing down if necessary to let the vehicle pass. Never obstruct drivers who wish to pass. Speeding up or driving unpredictably while someone is overtaking you is dangerous. Drop back to maintain a two-second gap if someone overtakes and pulls into the gap in front of you.

169 Do not hold up a long queue of traffic, especially if you are driving a large or slow-moving vehicle. Check your mirrors frequently, and if necessary, pull in where it is safe and let traffic pass.

Road junctions

 Take extra care at junctions. You should

- ◯ watch out for cyclists, motorcyclists, powered wheelchairs/mobility scooters and pedestrians as they are not always easy to see. Be aware that they may not have seen or heard you if you are approaching from behind
- ◯ watch out for pedestrians crossing a road into which you are turning. If they have started to cross they have priority, so give way
- ◯ watch out for long vehicles which may be turning at a junction ahead; they may have to use the whole width of the road to make the turn (see Rule 221)
- ◯ watch out for horse riders who may take a different line on the road from that which you would expect
- ◯ not assume, when waiting at a junction, that a vehicle coming from the right and signalling left will actually turn. Wait and make sure
- ◯ look all around before emerging. Do not cross or join a road until there is a gap large enough for you to do so safely.

Rule 170 – *Give way to pedestrians who have started to cross*

171 You **MUST** stop behind the line at a junction with a 'Stop' sign and a solid white line across the road. Wait for a safe gap in the traffic before you move off.
Laws RTA 1988 sect 36 & TSRGD regs 10 & 16

172 The approach to a junction may have a 'Give Way' sign or a triangle marked on the road. You **MUST** give way to traffic on the main road when emerging from a junction with broken white lines across the road.
Laws RTA 1988 sect 36 & TSRGD regs 10(1),16(1) & 25

Rule 173 – *Assess your vehicle's length and do not obstruct traffic*

173 **Dual carriageways.** When crossing or turning right, first assess whether the central reservation is deep enough to protect the full length of your vehicle.

○ If it is, then you should treat each half of the carriageway as a separate road. Wait in the central reservation until there is a safe gap in the traffic on the second half of the road.
○ If the central reservation is too shallow for the length of your vehicle, wait until you can cross both carriageways in one go.

174 **Box junctions.** These have criss-cross yellow lines painted on the road (see page 110). You **MUST NOT** enter the box until your exit road or lane is clear. However, you may enter the box and wait when you want to turn right, and are only stopped from doing so by oncoming traffic, or by other vehicles waiting to turn right. At signalled roundabouts you **MUST NOT** enter the box unless you can cross over it completely without stopping. Law TSRGD regs 10(1) & 29(2)

Rule 174 – *Enter a box junction only if your exit road is clear*

Junctions controlled by traffic lights

175 You **MUST** stop behind the white 'Stop' line across your side of the road unless the light is green. If the amber light appears you may go on only if you have already crossed the stop line or are so close to it that to stop might cause a collision.

Laws RTA 1988 sect 36 & TSRGD regs 10 & 36

176 You **MUST NOT** move forward over the white line when the red light is showing. Only go forward when the traffic lights are green if there is room for you to clear the junction safely or you are taking up a position to turn right. If the traffic lights are not working, treat the situation as you would an unmarked junction and proceed with great care.

Laws RTA 1988 sect 36 & TSRGD regs 10 & 36

177 **Green filter arrow.** This indicates a filter lane only. Do not enter that lane unless you want to go in the direction of the arrow. You may proceed in the direction of the green arrow when it, or the full green light shows. Give other traffic, especially cyclists, time and room to move into the correct lane.

178 **Advanced stop lines.** Some signal-controlled junctions have advanced stop lines to allow cycles to be positioned ahead of other traffic. Motorists, including motorcyclists, **MUST** stop at the first white line reached if the lights are amber or red and should avoid blocking the way or encroaching on the marked area at other times, e.g. if the junction ahead is blocked. If your vehicle has proceeded over the first white line at the time that the signal goes red, you **MUST** stop at the second white line, even if your vehicle is in the marked area. Allow cyclists time and space to move off when the green signal shows.

Laws RTA 1988 sect 36 & TSRGD regs 10, 36(1) & 43(2)

Rule 178 – Do not encroach on the cyclists' waiting area

Turning right

Well before you turn right you should

- use your mirrors to make sure you know the position and movement of traffic behind you
- give a right-turn signal
- take up a position just left of the middle of the road or in the space marked for traffic turning right
- leave room for other vehicles to pass on the left, if possible.

180 Wait until there is a safe gap between you and any oncoming vehicle. Watch out for cyclists, motorcyclists, pedestrians and other road users. Check your mirrors and blind spot again to make sure you are not being overtaken, then make the turn. Do not cut the corner. Take great care when turning into a main road; you will need to watch for traffic in both directions and wait for a safe gap.

Remember: Mirrors – Signal – Manoeuvre

Rule 180 – Position your vehicle correctly to avoid obstructing traffic

181 **When turning** right at crossroads where an oncoming vehicle is also turning right, there is a choice of two methods

- turn right side to right side; keep the other vehicle on your right and turn behind it. This is generally the safer method as you have a clear view of any approaching traffic when completing your turn

○ left side to left side, turning in front of each other. This can block your view of oncoming vehicles, so take extra care. Cyclists and motorcyclists in particular may be hidden from your view. Road layout, markings or how the other vehicle is positioned can determine which course should be taken.

Rule 181 – Left – Turning right side to right side. Right – Turning left side to left side.

Turning left

182 Use your mirrors and give a left-turn signal well before you turn left. Do not overtake just before you turn left and watch out for traffic coming up on your left before you make the turn, especially if driving a large vehicle. Cyclists, motorcyclists and other road users in particular may be hidden from your view.

Rule 182 – Do not cut in on cyclists

183 When turning

○ keep as close to the left as is safe and practicable
○ give way to any vehicles using a bus lane, cycle lane or tramway from either direction.

Roundabouts

184 **On approaching a roundabout** take notice and act on all the information available to you, including traffic signs, traffic lights and lane markings which direct you into the correct lane. You should

- ↻ use **Mirrors – Signal – Manoeuvre** at all stages
- ↻ decide as early as possible which exit you need to take
- ↻ give an appropriate signal (see Rule 186). Time your signals so as not to confuse other road users
- ↻ get into the correct lane
- ↻ adjust your speed and position to fit in with traffic conditions
- ↻ be aware of the speed and position of all the road users around you.

185 **When reaching the roundabout** you should

- ↻ give priority to traffic approaching from your right, unless directed otherwise by signs, road markings or traffic lights
- ↻ check whether road markings allow you to enter the roundabout without giving way. If so, proceed, but still look to the right before joining
- ↻ watch out for all other road users already on the roundabout; be aware they may not be signalling correctly or at all
- ↻ look forward before moving off to make sure traffic in front has moved off.

Rule 185 – Follow the correct procedure at roundabouts

186 **Signals and position.** When taking the first exit, unless signs or markings indicate otherwise

- ⟳ signal left and approach in the left-hand lane
- ⟳ keep to the left on the roundabout and continue signalling left to leave.

When taking an exit to the right or going full circle, unless signs or markings indicate otherwise

- ⟳ signal right and approach in the right-hand lane
- ⟳ keep to the right on the roundabout until you need to change lanes to exit the roundabout
- ⟳ signal left after you have passed the exit before the one you want.

When taking any intermediate exit, unless signs or markings indicate otherwise

- ⟳ select the appropriate lane on approach to and on the roundabout
- ⟳ you should not normally need to signal on approach
- ⟳ stay in this lane until you need to alter course to exit the roundabout
- ⟳ signal left after you have passed the exit before the one you want.

When there are more than three lanes at the entrance to a roundabout, use the most appropriate lane on approach and through it.

187 **In all cases watch out for** and give plenty of room to

- ⟳ pedestrians who may be crossing the approach and exit roads
- ⟳ traffic crossing in front of you on the roundabout, especially vehicles intending to leave by the next exit
- ⟳ traffic which may be straddling lanes or positioned incorrectly
- ⟳ motorcyclists
- ⟳ cyclists and horse riders who may stay in the left-hand lane and signal right if they intend to continue round the roundabout. Allow them to do so
- ⟳ long vehicles (including those towing trailers). These might have to take a different course or straddle lanes either approaching or on the roundabout because of their length. Watch out for their signals.

188 **Mini-roundabouts.** Approach these in the same way as normal roundabouts. All vehicles **MUST** pass round the central markings except large vehicles which are physically incapable of doing so. Remember, there is less space to manoeuvre and less time to signal. Avoid making U-turns at mini-roundabouts. Beware of others doing this.
Laws RTA 1988 sect 36 & TSRGD regs 10(1) & 16(1)

189 At double mini-roundabouts treat each roundabout separately and give way to traffic from the right.

190 **Multiple roundabouts.** At some complex junctions, there may be a series of mini-roundabouts at each intersection. Treat each mini-roundabout separately and follow the normal rules.

Rule 190 – *Treat each roundabout separately*

Pedestrian crossings

191 You **MUST NOT** park on a crossing or in the area covered by the zig-zag lines. You **MUST NOT** overtake the moving vehicle nearest the crossing or the vehicle nearest the crossing which has stopped to give way to pedestrians.
Laws ZPPPCRGD regs 18, 20 & 24, RTRA sect 25(5) & TSRGD regs 10, 27 & 28

61

In queuing traffic, you should keep the crossing clear.

Rule 192 – Keep the crossing clear

 You should take extra care where the view of either side of the crossing is blocked by queuing traffic or incorrectly parked vehicles. Pedestrians may be crossing between stationary vehicles.

 Allow pedestrians plenty of time to cross and do not harass them by revving your engine or edging forward.

 Zebra crossings. As you approach a zebra crossing

- ↪ look out for pedestrians waiting to cross and be ready to slow down or stop to let them cross
- ↪ you **MUST** give way when a pedestrian has moved onto a crossing
- ↪ allow more time for stopping on wet or icy roads
- ↪ do not wave or use your horn to invite pedestrians across; this could be dangerous if another vehicle is approaching
- ↪ be aware of pedestrians approaching from the side of the crossing.

A zebra crossing with a central island is two separate crossings (see pictures on page 10).

Law ZPPPCRGD reg 25

Signal-controlled crossings

196 **Pelican crossings.** These are signal-controlled crossings where flashing amber follows the red 'Stop' light. You **MUST** stop when the red light shows. When the amber light is flashing, you **MUST** give way to any pedestrians on the crossing. If the amber light is flashing and there are no pedestrians on the crossing, you may proceed with caution.

Laws ZPPPCRGD regs 23 & 26 & RTRA sect 25(5)

Rule 196 – *Allow pedestrians to cross when the amber light is flashing*

197 Pelican crossings which go straight across the road are one crossing, even when there is a central island. You **MUST** wait for pedestrians who are crossing from the other side of the island.

Laws ZPPPCRGD reg 26 & RTRA sect 25(5)

198 Give way to anyone still crossing after the signal for vehicles has changed to green. This advice applies to all crossings.

199 **Toucan, puffin and equestrian crossings.** These are similar to pelican crossings, but there is no flashing amber phase; the light sequence for traffic at these three crossings is the same as at traffic lights. If the signal-controlled crossing is not working, proceed with extreme caution.

Reversing

 200 Choose an appropriate place to manoeuvre. If you need to turn your vehicle around, wait until you find a safe place. Try not to reverse or turn round in a busy road; find a quiet side road or drive round a block of side streets.

 201 Do not reverse from a side road into a main road. When using a driveway, reverse in and drive out if you can.

 202 Look carefully before you start reversing. You should

- ⟲ use all your mirrors
- ⟲ check the 'blind spot' behind you (the part of the road you cannot see easily in the mirrors)
- ⟲ check there are no pedestrians (particularly children), cyclists, other road users or obstructions in the road behind you.

Rule 202 – Check all round when reversing

Reverse slowly while

- ⟲ checking all around
- ⟲ looking mainly through the rear window
- ⟲ being aware that the front of your vehicle will swing out as you turn.

Get someone to guide you if you cannot see clearly.

 203 You **MUST NOT** reverse your vehicle further than necessary.

Law CUR reg 106

64

Road users requiring extra care

204 The most vulnerable road users are pedestrians, cyclists, motorcyclists and horse riders. It is particularly important to be aware of children, older and disabled people, and learner and inexperienced drivers and riders.

Pedestrians

205 There is a risk of pedestrians, especially children, stepping unexpectedly into the road. You should drive with the safety of children in mind at a speed suitable for the conditions.

206 **Drive carefully and slowly** when

- in crowded shopping streets, Home Zones and Quiet Lanes (see Rule 218) or residential areas
- driving past bus and tram stops; pedestrians may emerge suddenly into the road
- passing parked vehicles, especially ice cream vans; children are more interested in ice cream than traffic and may run into the road unexpectedly
- needing to cross a pavement or cycle track; for example, to reach or leave a driveway. Give way to pedestrians and cyclists on the pavement
- reversing into a side road; look all around the vehicle and give way to any pedestrians who may be crossing the road
- turning at road junctions; give way to pedestrians who are already crossing the road into which you are turning
- the pavement is closed due to street repairs and pedestrians are directed to use the road
- approaching pedestrians on narrow rural roads without a footway or footpath. Always slow down and be prepared to stop if necessary, giving them plenty of room as you drive past.

Rule 206 – *Watch out for children in busy areas*

 Particularly vulnerable pedestrians. These include

- ⟳ children and older pedestrians who may not be able to judge your speed and could step into the road in front of you. At 40 mph (64 km/h) your vehicle will probably kill any pedestrians it hits. At 20 mph (32 km/h) there is only a 1 in 20 chance of the pedestrian being killed. So kill your speed
- ⟳ older pedestrians who may need more time to cross the road. Be patient and allow them to cross in their own time. Do not hurry them by revving your engine or edging forward
- ⟳ people with disabilities. People with hearing impairments may not be aware of your vehicle approaching. Those with walking difficulties require more time
- ⟳ blind or partially sighted people, who may be carrying a white cane using a guide dog. They may not be able to see you approaching
- ⟳ deafblind people who may be carrying a white cane with a red band or using a dog with a red and white harness. They may not see or hear instructions or signals.

 Near schools. Drive slowly and be particularly aware of young cyclists and pedestrians. In some places, there may be a flashing amber signal below the 'School' warning sign which tells you that there may be children crossing the road ahead. Drive very slowly until you are clear of the area.

 Drive carefully and slowly when passing a stationary bus showing a 'School Bus' sign (see page 111) as children may be getting on or off.

You **MUST** stop when a school crossing patrol shows a 'Stop for children' sign (see pages 98 & 100).
Law RTRA sect 28

Motorcyclists and cyclists

 It is often difficult to see motorcyclists and cyclists, especially when they are coming up from behind, coming out of junctions, at roundabouts, overtaking you or filtering through traffic. Always look out for them before you emerge from a junction; they could be approaching faster than you think. When turning right across a line of slow-moving or stationary traffic, look out for cyclists or motorcyclists on the inside of the traffic you are crossing. Be especially careful when turning, and when changing direction or lane. Be sure to check mirrors and blind spots carefully.

Rule 211 – Look out for motorcyclists and cyclists at junctions

 When passing motorcyclists and cyclists, give them plenty of room (see Rules162–167). If they look over their shoulder it could mean that they intend to pull out, turn right or change direction. Give them time and space to do so.

213 Motorcyclists and cyclists may suddenly need to avoid uneven road surfaces and obstacles such as drain covers or oily, wet or icy patches on the road. Give them plenty of room and pay particular attention to any sudden change of direction they may have to make.

Other road users

214 **Animals.** When passing animals, drive slowly. Give them plenty of room and be ready to stop. Do not scare animals by sounding your horn, revving your engine or accelerating rapidly once you have passed them. Look out for animals being led, driven or ridden on the road and take extra care. Keep your speed down at bends and on narrow country roads. If a road is blocked by a herd of animals, stop and switch off your engine until they have left the road. Watch out for animals on unfenced roads.

215 **Horse riders and horse-drawn vehicles.** Be particularly careful of horse riders and horse-drawn vehicles especially when overtaking. Always pass wide and slowly. Horse riders are often children, so take extra care and remember riders may ride in double file when escorting a young or inexperienced horse or rider. Look out for horse riders' and horse drivers' signals and heed a request to slow down or stop. Take great care and treat all horses as a potential hazard; they can be unpredictable, despite the efforts of their rider/driver.

216 **Older drivers.** Their reactions may be slower than other drivers. Make allowance for this.

217 **Learners and inexperienced drivers.** They may not be so skilful at anticipating and responding to events. Be particularly patient with learner drivers and young drivers. Drivers who have recently passed their test may display a 'new driver' plate or sticker (see Annex 8 – Safety code for new drivers).

218 **Home Zones and Quiet Lanes.** These are places where people could be using the whole of the road for a range of activities such as children playing or for a community event. You should drive slowly and carefully and be prepared to stop to allow people extra time to make space for you to pass them in safety.

Other vehicles

 Emergency and Incident Support vehicles. You should look and listen for ambulances, fire engines, police, doctors or other emergency vehicles using flashing blue, red or green lights and sirens or flashing headlights, or Highways Agency Traffic Officer and Incident Support vehicles using flashing amber lights. When one approaches do not panic. Consider the route of such a vehicle and take appropriate action to let it pass, while complying with all traffic signs. If necessary, pull to the side of the road and stop, but try to avoid stopping before the brow of a hill, a bend or narrow section of road. Do not endanger yourself, other road users or pedestrians and avoid mounting the kerb. Do not brake harshly on approach to a junction or roundabout, as a following vehicle may not have the same view as you.

Powered vehicles used by disabled people. These small vehicles travel at a maximum speed of 8 mph (12 km/h). On a dual carriageway where the speed limit exceeds 50 mph (80 km/h) they **MUST** have a flashing amber beacon, but on other roads you may not have that advance warning (see Rules 36–46 inclusive).

Law RVLR reg 17(1) & 26

Large vehicles. These may need extra road space to turn or to deal with a hazard that you are not able to see. If you are following a large vehicle, such as a bus or articulated lorry, be aware that the driver may not be able to see you in the mirrors. Be prepared to stop and wait if it needs room or time to turn.

***Rule 221** – Large vehicles need extra room*

222 Large vehicles can block your view. Your ability to see and to plan ahead will be improved if you pull back to increase your separation distance. Be patient, as larger vehicles are subject to lower speed limits than cars and motorcycles. Many large vehicles may be fitted with speed limiting devices which will restrict speed to 56 mph (90 km/h) even on a motorway.

223 **Buses, coaches and trams.** Give priority to these vehicles when you can do so safely, especially when they signal to pull away from stops. Look out for people getting off a bus or tram and crossing the road.

224 **Electric vehicles.** Be careful of electric vehicles such as milk floats and trams. Trams move quickly but silently and cannot steer to avoid you.

225 **Vehicles with flashing amber beacons.** These warn of a slow-moving or stationary vehicle (such as a Traffic Officer vehicle, salt spreader, snow plough or recovery vehicle) or abnormal loads, so approach with caution. On unrestricted dual carriageways, motor vehicles first used on or after 1 January 1947 with a maximum speed of 25 mph (40 km/h) or less (such as tractors) **MUST** use a flashing amber beacon (also see Rule 220).

Law RVLR 1989, reg 17

226 You **MUST** use headlights when visibility is seriously reduced, generally when you cannot see for more than 100 metres (328 feet). You may also use front or rear fog lights but you **MUST** switch them off when visibility improves (see Rule 236).
Law RVLR regs 25 & 27

227 **Wet weather.** In wet weather, stopping distances will be at least double those required for stopping on dry roads (see pages 38–39). This is because your tyres have less grip on the road. In wet weather

- you should keep well back from the vehicle in front. This will increase your ability to see and plan ahead
- if the steering becomes unresponsive, it probably means that water is preventing the tyres from gripping the road. Ease off the accelerator and slow down gradually
- the rain and spray from vehicles may make it difficult to see and be seen
- be aware of the dangers of spilt diesel that will make the surface very slippery (see Annex 6)
- take extra care around pedestrians, cyclists, motorcyclists and horse riders.

Icy and snowy weather

228 In winter check the local weather forecast for warnings of icy or snowy weather. **DO NOT** drive in these conditions unless your journey is essential. If it is, take great care and allow more time for your journey. Take an emergency kit of de-icer and ice scraper, torch, warm clothing and boots, first aid kit, jump leads and a shovel, together with a warm drink and emergency food in case you get stuck or your vehicle breaks down.

Before you set off

○ you **MUST** be able to see, so clear all snow and ice from all your windows

○ you **MUST** ensure that lights are clean and number plates are clearly visible and legible

○ make sure the mirrors are clear and the windows are demisted thoroughly

○ remove all snow that might fall off into the path of other road users

○ check your planned route is clear of delays and that no further snowfalls or severe weather are predicted.

Laws CUR reg 30, RVLR reg 23, VERA sect 43 & RV(DRM)R reg 11

Rule 229 – *Make sure your windscreen is completely clear*

230 **When driving** in icy or snowy weather

- ↻ drive with care, even if the roads have been treated
- ↻ keep well back from the road user in front as stopping distances can be ten times greater than on dry roads
- ↻ take care when overtaking vehicles spreading salt or other de-icer, particularly if you are riding a motorcycle or cycle
- ↻ watch out for snowploughs which may throw out snow on either side. Do not overtake them unless the lane you intend to use has been cleared
- ↻ be prepared for the road conditions to change over relatively short distances
- ↻ listen to travel bulletins and take note of variable message signs that may provide information about weather, road and traffic conditions ahead.

231 **Drive extremely carefully** when the roads are icy. Avoid sudden actions as these could cause loss of control. You should

- ↻ drive at a slow speed in as high a gear as possible; accelerate and brake very gently
- ↻ drive particularly slowly on bends where loss of control is more likely. Brake progressively on the straight before you reach a bend. Having slowed down, steer smoothly round the bend, avoiding sudden actions
- ↻ check your grip on the road surface when there is snow or ice by choosing a safe place to brake gently. If the steering feels unresponsive this may indicate ice and your vehicle losing its grip on the road. When travelling on ice, tyres make virtually no noise.

Windy weather

232 High-sided vehicles are most affected by windy weather, but strong gusts can also blow a car, cyclist, motorcyclist or horse rider off course. This can happen on open stretches of road exposed to strong crosswinds, or when passing bridges or gaps in hedges.

233 In very windy weather your vehicle may be affected by turbulence created by large vehicles. Motorcyclists are particularly affected, so keep well back from them when they are overtaking a high-sided vehicle.

Fog

234 **Before entering fog** check your mirrors then slow down. If the word 'Fog' is shown on a roadside signal but the road is clear, be prepared for a bank of fog or drifting patchy fog ahead. Even if it seems to be clearing, you can suddenly find yourself in thick fog.

235 **When driving in fog** you should

- ⮑ use your lights as required (see Rule 226)
- ⮑ keep a safe distance behind the vehicle in front. Rear lights can give a false sense of security
- ⮑ be able to pull up well within the distance you can see clearly. This is particularly important on motorways and dual carriageways, as vehicles are travelling faster
- ⮑ use your windscreen wipers and demisters
- ⮑ beware of other drivers not using headlights
- ⮑ not accelerate to get away from a vehicle which is too close behind you
- ⮑ check your mirrors before you slow down. Then use your brakes so that your brake lights warn drivers behind you that you are slowing down
- ⮑ stop in the correct position at a junction with limited visibility and listen for traffic. When you are sure it is safe to emerge, do so positively and do not hesitate in a position that puts you directly in the path of approaching vehicles.

236 You **MUST NOT** use front or rear fog lights unless visibility is seriously reduced (see Rule 226) as they dazzle other road users and can obscure your brake lights. You **MUST** switch them off when visibility improves.

Law RVLR regs 25 & 27

237 **Hot weather.** Keep your vehicle well ventilated to avoid drowsiness. Be aware that the road surface may become soft or if it rains after a dry spell it may become slippery. These conditions could affect your steering and braking. If you are dazzled by bright sunlight, slow down and if necessary, stop.

You **MUST NOT** wait or park on yellow lines during the times of operation shown on nearby time plates (or zone entry signs if in a Controlled Parking Zone) – see pages 106 and 109. Double yellow lines indicate a prohibition of waiting at any time even if there are no upright signs. You **MUST NOT** wait or park, or stop to set down and pick up passengers, on school entrance markings (see page 110) when upright signs indicate a prohibition of stopping.

Law RTRA sects 5 & 8

Parking

 Use off-street parking areas, or bays marked out with white lines on the road as parking places, wherever possible. If you have to stop on the roadside

⊙ do not park facing against the traffic flow

⊙ stop as close as you can to the side

⊙ do not stop too close to a vehicle displaying a Blue Badge: remember, the occupant may need more room to get in or out

⊙ you **MUST** switch off the engine, headlights and fog lights

⊙ you **MUST** apply the handbrake before leaving the vehicle

Rule 239 – Check before opening your door

○ you **MUST** ensure you do not hit anyone when you open your door. Check for cyclists or other traffic

○ it is safer for your passengers (especially children) to get out of the vehicle on the side next to the kerb

○ put all valuables out of sight and make sure your vehicle is secure

○ lock your vehicle.

Laws CUR reg 98, 105 & 107, RVLR reg 27 & RTA 1988 sect 42

240 You **MUST NOT** stop or park on

○ the carriageway or the hard shoulder of a motorway except in an emergency (see Rule 270)

○ a pedestrian crossing, including the area marked by the zig-zag lines (see Rule 191)

○ a clearway (see page 101)

○ taxi bays as indicated by upright signs and markings

○ an Urban Clearway within its hours of operation, except to pick up or set down passengers (see page 101)

○ a road marked with double white lines, even when a broken white line is on your side of the road, except to pick up or set down passengers, or to load or unload goods

○ a tram or cycle lane during its period of operation

○ a cycle track

○ red lines, in the case of specially designated 'red routes', unless otherwise indicated by signs.

Any vehicle may enter a bus lane to stop, load or unload where this is not prohibited (see Rule 141).

Laws MT(E&W)R regs 7 & 9, MT(S)R regs 6 & 8, ZPPPCRGD regs 18 & 20, RTRA sects 5, 6 & 8, TSRGD regs 10, 26 & 27, RTA 1988 sects 21(1) & 36

241 You **MUST NOT** park in parking spaces reserved for specific users, such as Blue Badge holders, residents or motorcycles, unless entitled to do so.

Laws CSDPA sect 21 & RTRA sects 5 & 8

242 You **MUST NOT** leave your vehicle or trailer in a dangerous position or where it causes any unnecessary obstruction of the road.

Laws RTA 1988, sect 22 & CUR reg 103

243

DO NOT stop or park

- ◯ near a school entrance
- ◯ anywhere you would prevent access for Emergency Services
- ◯ at or near a bus or tram stop or taxi rank
- ◯ on the approach to a level crossing/tramway crossing
- ◯ opposite or within 10 metres (32 feet) of a junction, except in an authorised parking space
- ◯ near the brow of a hill or hump bridge
- ◯ opposite a traffic island or (if this would cause an obstruction) another parked vehicle
- ◯ where you would force other traffic to enter a tram lane
- ◯ where the kerb has been lowered to help wheelchair users and powered mobility vehicles
- ◯ in front of an entrance to a property
- ◯ on a bend
- ◯ where you would obstruct cyclists' use of cycle facilities *except* when forced to do so by stationary traffic.

244

You **MUST NOT** park partially or wholly on the pavement in London, and should not do so elsewhere unless signs permit it. Parking on the pavement can obstruct and seriously inconvenience pedestrians, people in wheelchairs or with visual impairments and people with prams or pushchairs.

Law GL(GP)A sect 15

245

Controlled Parking Zones. The zone entry signs indicate the times when the waiting restrictions within the zone are in force. Parking may be allowed in some places at other times. Otherwise parking will be within separately signed and marked bays.

246

Goods vehicles. Vehicles with a maximum laden weight of over 7.5 tonnes (including any trailer) **MUST NOT** be parked on a verge, pavement or any land situated between carriageways, without police permission. The only exception is when parking is essential for loading and unloading, in which case the vehicle **MUST NOT** be left unattended.

Law RTA 1988 sect 19

Loading and unloading. Do not load or unload where there are yellow markings on the kerb and upright signs advise restrictions are in place (see pages 109–110). This may be permitted where parking is otherwise restricted. On red routes, specially marked and signed bays indicate where and when loading and unloading is permitted.

Law RTRA sects 5 & 8

Parking at night

You **MUST NOT** park on a road at night facing against the direction of the traffic flow unless in a recognised parking space.

Laws CUR reg 101 & RVLR reg 24

All vehicles **MUST** display parking lights when parked on a road or a lay-by on a road with a speed limit greater than 30 mph (48 km/h).

Law RVLR reg 24

Cars, goods vehicles not exceeding 1525 kg unladen weight, invalid carriages, motorcycles and pedal cycles may be parked without lights on a road (or lay-by) with a speed limit of 30 mph (48 km/h) or less if they are

- ⊃ at least 10 metres (32 feet) away from any junction, close to the kerb and facing in the direction of the traffic flow
- ⊃ in a recognised parking place or lay-by.

Other vehicles and trailers, and all vehicles with projecting loads, MUST NOT be left on a road at night without lights.

Laws RVLR reg 24 & CUR reg 82(7)

Parking in fog. It is especially dangerous to park on the road in fog. If it is unavoidable, leave your parking lights or sidelights on.

252 **Parking on hills.** If you park on a hill
you should

- ⊖ park close to the kerb and apply the
  handbrake firmly
- ⊖ select a forward gear and turn your
  steering wheel away from the kerb
  when facing uphill
- ⊖ select reverse gear and turn your
  steering wheel towards the kerb
  when facing downhill
- ⊖ use 'park' if your car has an
  automatic gearbox.

facing downhill

facing uphill

Rule 252 – *Turn your wheels away from the
kerb when parking facing uphill. Turn them
towards the kerb when parking facing downhill*

Decriminalised Parking Enforcement (DPE)

DPE is becoming increasingly common as more
authorities take on this role. The local traffic authority
assumes responsibility for enforcing many parking
contraventions in place of the police. Further details
on DPE may be found at the following websites:

www.parking-appeals.gov.uk (outside London)
www.parkingandtrafficappeals.gov.uk (inside London)

Motorways

Many other Rules apply to motorway driving, either wholly or in part: Rules 46, 57, 83–126, 130–134, 139, 144, 146–151, 160, 161, 219, 221–222, 225, 226–237, 274–278, 280, and 281–290.

General

253 **Prohibited vehicles.** Motorways **MUST NOT** be used by pedestrians, holders of provisional motorcycle or car licences, riders of motorcycles under 50 cc, cyclists, horse riders, certain slow-moving vehicles and those carrying oversized loads (except by special permission), agricultural vehicles, and powered wheelchairs/ powered mobility scooters (see Rules 36–46 incl)

Laws HA 1980 sects 16, 17 & sch 4, MT(E&W)R regs 3(d), 4 & 11, MT(E&W)(A)R, R(S)A sects 7, 8 & sch 3, RTRA sects 17(2) & (3), & MT(S)R reg 10

254 Traffic on motorways usually travels faster than on other roads, so you have less time to react. It is especially important to use your mirrors earlier and look much further ahead than you would on other roads.

Motorway signals

255 Motorway signals (see page 96) are used to warn you of a danger ahead. For example, there may be an incident, fog, a spillage or road workers on the carriageway which you may not immediately be able to see.

256 Signals situated on the central reservation apply to all lanes. On very busy stretches, signals may be overhead with a separate signal for each lane.

257 **Amber flashing lights.** These warn of a hazard ahead. The signal may show a temporary maximum speed limit, lanes that are closed or a message such as 'Fog'. Adjust your speed and look out for the danger until you pass a signal which is not flashing or one that gives the 'All clear' sign and you are sure it is safe to increase your speed.

258 **Red flashing lights.** If red lights on the overhead signals flash above your lane and a red 'X' is showing, you **MUST NOT** go beyond the signal in that lane. If red lights flash on a signal in the central reservation or at the side of the road, you **MUST NOT** go beyond the signal in any lane.

Laws RTA 1988 sect 36 & TSRGD regs 10 & 38

Driving on the motorway

259 **Joining the motorway.** When you join the motorway you will normally approach it from a road on the left (a slip road) or from an adjoining motorway. You should

- give priority to traffic already on the motorway
- check the traffic on the motorway and match your speed to fit safely into the traffic flow in the left-hand lane
- not cross solid white lines that separate lanes or use the hard shoulder
- stay on the slip road if it continues as an extra lane on the motorway
- remain in the left-hand lane long enough to adjust to the speed of traffic before considering overtaking.

On the motorway

260 When you can see well ahead and the road conditions are good, you should

- drive at a steady cruising speed which you and your vehicle can handle safely and is within the speed limit (see table on page 37)
- keep a safe distance from the vehicle in front and increase the gap on wet or icy roads, or in fog (see Rules 126 and 235).

261 You **MUST NOT** exceed 70 mph (112 km/h), or the maximum speed limit permitted for your vehicle (see page 37). If a lower speed limit is in force, either permanently or temporarily, at road works for example, you **MUST NOT** exceed the lower limit. On some motorways, mandatory motorway signals (which display the speed within a red ring) are used to vary the maximum speed limit to improve traffic flow. You **MUST NOT** exceed this speed limit.

Law RTRA sects 17, 86, 89 & sch 6

The monotony of driving on a motorway can make you feel sleepy. To minimise the risk, follow the advice in Rule 91.

 You **MUST NOT** reverse, cross the central reservation, or drive against the traffic flow. If you have missed your exit, or have taken the wrong route, carry on to the next exit.

Laws MT(E&W)R regs 6, 8 & 10 & MT(S)R regs 4, 5, 7 & 9

Lane discipline

 You should always drive in the left-hand lane when the road ahead is clear. If you are overtaking a number of slower-moving vehicles, you should return to the left-hand lane as soon as you are safely past. Slow-moving or speed-restricted vehicles should always remain in the left-hand lane of the carriageway unless overtaking. You **MUST NOT** drive on the hard shoulder except in an emergency or if directed to do so by the police, HA traffic officers in uniform or by signs.

Laws MT(E&W)R regs 5, 9 & 16(1)(a), MT(S)R regs 4, 8 & 14(1)(a), and RTA 1988, sects 35 & 186, as amended by TMA 2004 sect 6

The right-hand lane of a motorway with three or more lanes **MUST NOT** be used (except in prescribed circumstances) if you are driving

- ➲ any vehicle drawing a trailer
- ➲ a goods vehicle with a maximum laden weight exceeding 3.5 tonnes but not exceeding 7.5 tonnes, which is required to be fitted with a speed limiter
- ➲ a goods vehicle with a maximum laden weight exceeding 7.5 tonnes
- ➲ a passenger vehicle with a maximum laden weight exceeding 7.5 tonnes constructed or adapted to carry more than eight seated passengers in addition to the driver
- ➲ a passenger vehicle with a maximum laden weight not exceeding 7.5 tonnes which is constructed or adapted to carry more than eight seated passengers in addition to the driver, which is required to be fitted with a speed limiter.

Laws MT(E&W)R reg 12, MT(E&W)AR (2004), MT(S)R reg 11 & MT(S)AR (2004)

266 **Approaching a junction.** Look well ahead for signals or signs. Direction signs may be placed over the road. If you need to change lanes, do so in good time. At some junctions a lane may lead directly off the motorway. Only get in that lane if you wish to go in the direction indicated on the overhead signs.

Overtaking

267 Do not overtake unless you are sure it is safe and legal to do so. Overtake only on the right. You should

- check your mirrors
- take time to judge the speeds correctly
- make sure that the lane you will be joining is sufficiently clear ahead and behind
- take a quick sideways glance into the blind spot area to verify the position of a vehicle that may have disappeared from your view in the mirror
- remember that traffic may be coming up behind you very quickly. Check all your mirrors carefully. Look out for motorcyclists. When it is safe to do so, signal in plenty of time, then move out
- ensure you do not cut in on the vehicle you have overtaken
- be especially careful at night and in poor visibility when it is harder to judge speed and distance.

268 Do not overtake on the left or move to a lane on your left to overtake. In congested conditions, where adjacent lanes of traffic are moving at similar speeds, traffic in left-hand lanes may sometimes be moving faster than traffic to the right. In these conditions you may keep up with the traffic in your lane even if this means passing traffic in the lane to your right. Do not weave in and out of lanes to overtake.

269 **Hard shoulder.** You **MUST NOT** use the hard shoulder for overtaking. In areas where an Active Traffic Management (ATM) Scheme is in force, the hard shoulder may be used as a running lane. You will know when you can use this because a speed limit sign will be shown above all open lanes, including the hard shoulder. A red cross or blank sign above the hard shoulder means that you **MUST NOT** drive on the hard shoulder except in an emergency or breakdown. Emergency refuge areas have also been built into these areas for use in cases of emergency or breakdown.

Laws MT(E&W)R regs 5, 5A & 9, MT(S)R regs 4 & 8

Rule 269 – *Overhead gantry showing red cross over hard shoulder*

Stopping

270 You **MUST NOT** stop on the carriageway, hard shoulder, slip road, central reservation or verge except in an emergency, or when told to do so by the police, HA traffic officers in uniform, an emergency sign or by flashing red light signals. Do not stop on the hard shoulder to either make or receive mobile phone calls.

Laws MT(E&W)R regs 5A, 7, 9, 10 & 16,MT(S)R regs 6(1), 8, 9 & 14, PRA 2002 sect 41 & sched 5(8), & RTA 1988 sects 35 & 163 as amended by TMA 2004, sect 6

271 You **MUST NOT** pick up or set down anyone, or walk on a motorway, except in an emergency.

Laws RTRA sect 17 & MT(E&W)R reg 15

Leaving the motorway

272 Unless signs indicate that a lane leads directly off the motorway, you will normally leave the motorway by a slip road on your left. You should

- ➲ watch for the signs letting you know you are getting near your exit
- ➲ move into the left-hand lane well before reaching your exit
- ➲ signal left in good time and reduce your speed on the slip road as necessary.

273 On leaving the motorway or using a link road between motorways, your speed may be higher than you realise – 50 mph may feel like 30 mph. Check your speedometer and adjust your speed accordingly. Some slip-roads and link roads have sharp bends, so you will need to slow down.

Breakdowns & incidents

Breakdowns

274 If your vehicle breaks down, think first of all other road users and

- ○ get your vehicle off the road if possible
- ○ warn other traffic by using your hazard warning lights if your vehicle is causing an obstruction
- ○ help other road users see you by wearing light-coloured or fluorescent clothing in daylight and reflective clothing at night or in poor visibility
- ○ put a warning triangle on the road at least 45 metres (147 feet) behind your broken-down vehicle on the same side of the road, or use other permitted warning devices if you have them. Always take great care when placing or retrieving them, but never use them on motorways
- ○ if possible, keep your sidelights on if it is dark or visibility is poor
- ○ do not stand (or let anybody else stand) between your vehicle and oncoming traffic
- ○ at night or in poor visibility do not stand where you will prevent other road users seeing your lights.

Additional rules for the motorway

275 If your vehicle develops a problem, leave the motorway at the next exit or pull into a service area. If you cannot do so, you should

- ○ pull on to the hard shoulder and stop as far to the left as possible, with your wheels turned to the left
- ○ try to stop near an emergency telephone (situated at approximately one-mile intervals along the hard shoulder)
- ○ leave the vehicle by the left-hand door and ensure your passengers do the same. You **MUST** leave any animals in the vehicle or, in an emergency, keep them under proper control on the verge. Never attempt to place a warning triangle on a motorway

Rule 275 – *Keep well back from the hard shoulder*

- do not put yourself in danger by attempting even simple repairs
- ensure that passengers keep away from the carriageway and hard shoulder, and that children are kept under control
- walk to an emergency telephone on your side of the carriageway (follow the arrows on the posts at the back of the hard shoulder) – the telephone is free of charge and connects directly to the Highways Agency or the police. Use these in preference to a mobile phone (see Rule 283). Always face the traffic when you speak on the phone
- give full details to the Highways Agency or the police; also inform them if you are a vulnerable motorist such as disabled, older or travelling alone
- return and wait near your vehicle (well away from the carriageway and hard shoulder)
- if you feel at risk from another person, return to your vehicle by a left-hand door and lock all doors. Leave your vehicle again as soon as you feel this danger has passed.

Laws MT(E&W)R reg 14 & MT(S)R reg 12

276 Before you rejoin the carriageway after a breakdown, build up speed on the hard shoulder and watch for a safe gap in the traffic. Be aware that other vehicles may be stationary on the hard shoulder.

If you cannot get your vehicle onto the hard shoulder

- ➲ do not attempt to place any warning device on the carriageway
- ➲ switch on your hazard warning lights
- ➲ leave your vehicle only when you can safely get clear of the carriageway.

 Disabled drivers. If you have a disability which prevents you from following the above advice you should

- ➲ stay in your vehicle
- ➲ switch on your hazard warning lights
- ➲ display a 'Help' pennant or, if you have a car or mobile telephone, contact the emergency services and be prepared to advise them of your location.

Obstructions

279 If anything falls from your vehicle (or any other vehicle) on to the road, stop and retrieve it only if it is safe to do so.

280 **Motorways.** On a motorway do not try to remove the obstruction yourself. Stop at the next emergency telephone and call the Highways Agency or the police.

Incidents

281 **Warning signs or flashing lights.** If you see or hear emergency or incident support vehicles in the distance, be aware there may be an incident ahead (see Rule 219). Police Officers and Highways Agency Traffic Officers may be required to work in the carriageway, for example dealing with debris, collisions or conducting rolling road blocks. Police officers will use rear-facing flashing red and blue lights and HA Traffic Officers will use rear-facing flashing red and amber lights in these situations. Watch out for such signals, slow down and be prepared to stop. You **MUST** follow any directions given by Police officers or Traffic officers as to whether you can safely pass the incident or blockage.

Laws RTA1988, sects 35 &163, and as amended by TMA 2004, sect 6

282 When passing the scene of an incident or crash do not be distracted or slow down unnecessarily (for example if an incident is on the other side of a dual carriageway). This may cause a collision or traffic congestion, but see Rule 283.

283 If you are involved in a crash or stop to give assistance

- �𝗈 use your hazard warning lights to warn other traffic
- �𝗈 ask drivers to switch off their engines and stop smoking
- �𝗈 arrange for the emergency services to be called immediately with full details of the incident location and any casualties (on a motorway, use the emergency telephone which allows easy location by the emergency services. If you use a mobile phone, first make sure you have identified your location from the marker posts on the side of the hard shoulder)
- �𝗈 move uninjured people away from the vehicles to safety; on a motorway this should, if possible, be well away from the traffic, the hard shoulder and the central reservation
- ◑ do not move injured people from their vehicles unless they are in immediate danger from fire or explosion
- ◑ do not remove a motorcyclist's helmet unless it is essential to do so
- ◑ be prepared to give first aid as shown on pages 125–127
- ◑ stay at the scene until emergency services arrive.

If you are involved in any other medical emergency on the motorway you should contact the emergency services in the same way.

Incidents involving dangerous goods

284 Vehicles carrying dangerous goods in packages will be marked with plain orange reflective plates. Road tankers and vehicles carrying tank containers of dangerous goods will have hazard warning plates (see page 111).

285 If an incident involves a vehicle containing dangerous goods, follow the advice in Rule 283 and, in particular

- switch off engines and **DO NOT SMOKE**
- keep well away from the vehicle and do not be tempted to try to rescue casualties as you yourself could become one
- call the emergency services and give as much information as possible about the labels and markings on the vehicle. **DO NOT** use a mobile phone close to a vehicle carrying flammable loads.

Documentation

286 If you are involved in a collision which causes damage or injury to any other person, vehicle, animal or property, you **MUST**

- stop
- give your own and the vehicle owner's name and address, and the registration number of the vehicle, to anyone having reasonable grounds for requiring them
- if you do not give your name and address at the time of the collision, report it to the police as soon as reasonably practicable, and in any case within 24 hours.

Law RTA 1988 sect 170

287 If another person is injured and you do not produce your insurance certificate at the time of the crash to a police officer or to anyone having reasonable grounds to request it, you **MUST**

- report it to the police as soon as possible and in any case within 24 hours
- produce your insurance certificate for the police within seven days.

Law RTA 1988 sect 170

288 When the 'Road Works Ahead' sign is displayed, you will need to be more watchful and look for additional signs providing more specific instructions. Observe all signs – they are there for your safety and the safety of road workers.

- You **MUST NOT** exceed any temporary maximum speed limit.
- Use your mirrors and get into the correct lane for your vehicle in good time and as signs direct.
- Do not switch lanes to overtake queuing traffic.
- Take extra care near cyclists and motorcyclists as they are vulnerable to skidding on grit, mud or other debris at road works.
- Where lanes are restricted due to road works, merge in turn (see Rule 134).
- Do not drive through an area marked off by traffic cones.
- Watch out for traffic entering or leaving the works area, but do not be distracted by what is going on there. Concentrate on the road ahead, not the road works.
- Bear in mind that the road ahead may be obstructed by the works or by slow moving or stationary traffic.
- Keep a safe distance – there could be queues in front.

To obtain further information about road works see page 129.

Law RTRA sect 16

Additional rules for high-speed roads

289 Take special care on motorways and other high-speed dual carriageways.

- ⊙ One or more lanes may be closed to traffic and a lower speed limit may apply.
- ⊙ Works vehicles that are slow moving or stationary with a large 'Keep Left' or 'Keep Right' sign on the back are sometimes used to close lanes for repairs, and a flashing light arrow may also be used to make the works vehicle more conspicuous from a distance and give earlier warning to drivers that they need to move over to the next lane.
- ⊙ Check mirrors, slow down and change lanes if necessary.
- ⊙ Keep a safe distance from the vehicle in front (see Rule 126).

290 Contraflow systems mean that you may be travelling in a narrower lane than normal and with no permanent barrier between you and oncoming traffic. The hard shoulder may be used for traffic, but be aware that there may be broken-down vehicles ahead of you. Keep a good distance from the vehicle ahead and observe any temporary speed limits.

291 A level crossing is where a road crosses a railway or tramway line. Approach and cross it with care. Never drive onto a crossing until the road is clear on the other side and do not get too close to the car in front. Never stop or park on, or near, a crossing.

292 **Overhead electric lines.** It is dangerous to touch overhead electric lines. You **MUST** obey the safe height warning road signs and you should not continue forward onto the railway if your vehicle touches any height barrier or bells. The clearance available is usually 5 metres (16 feet 6 inches) but may be lower.

Laws RTA 1988 sect 36, TSRGD 2002 reg 17(5)

293 **Controlled Crossings.** Most crossings have traffic light signals with a steady amber light, twin flashing red stop lights (see pages 96 & 103) and an audible alarm for pedestrians. They may have full, half or no barriers.

- ⮑ You **MUST** always obey the flashing red stop lights.
- ⮑ You **MUST** stop behind the white line across the road.
- ⮑ Keep going if you have already crossed the white line when the amber light comes on.
- ⮑ Do not reverse onto or over a controlled crossing.
- ⮑ You **MUST** wait if a train goes by and the red lights continue to flash. This means another train will be passing soon.
- ⮑ Only cross when the lights go off and barriers open.
- ⮑ Never zig-zag around half-barriers, they lower automatically because a train is approaching.
- ⮑ At crossings where there are no barriers, a train is approaching when the lights show.

Laws RTA 1988 sect 36 & TSRGD regs 10 & 40

Rule 293 – Stop when the traffic lights show

Railway telephones. If you are driving a large or slow-moving vehicle, a long, low vehicle with a risk of grounding, or herding animals, a train could arrive before you are clear of the crossing. You **MUST** obey any sign instructing you to use the railway telephone to obtain permission to cross. You **MUST** also telephone when clear of the crossing if requested to do so.
Laws RTA 1988 sect 36 & TSRGD regs 10 & 16(1)

 Crossings without traffic lights. Vehicles should stop and wait at the barrier or gate when it begins to close and not cross until the barrier or gate opens.

 User-operated gates or barriers. Some crossings have 'Stop' signs and small red and green lights. You **MUST NOT** cross when the red light is showing, only cross if the green light is on. If crossing with a vehicle, you should

- open the gates or barriers on both sides of the crossing
- check that the green light is still on and cross quickly
- close the gates or barriers when you are clear of the crossing.
Laws RTA 1988 sect 36 & TSRGD regs 10 & 52(2)

 If there are no lights, follow the procedure in Rule 295. Stop, look both ways and listen before you cross. If there is a railway telephone, always use it to contact the signal operator to make sure it is safe to cross. Inform the signal operator again when you are clear of the crossing.

 Open crossings. These have no gates, barriers, attendant or traffic lights but will have a 'Give Way' sign. You should look both ways, listen and make sure there is no train coming before you cross.

Incidents and breakdowns. If your vehicle breaks down, or if you have an incident on a crossing you should

- get everyone out of the vehicle and clear of the crossing immediately
- use a railway telephone if available to tell the signal operator. Follow the instructions you are given
- move the vehicle clear of the crossing if there is time before a train arrives. If the alarm sounds, or the amber light comes on, leave the vehicle and get clear of the crossing immediately.

300 You **MUST NOT** enter a road, lane or other route reserved for trams. Take extra care where trams run along the road. You should avoid driving directly on top of the rails and should take care where trams leave the main carriageway to enter the reserved route, to ensure you do not follow them. The width taken up by trams is often shown by tram lanes marked by white lines, yellow dots or by a different type of road surface. Diamond-shaped signs and white light signals give instructions to tram drivers only.

Law RTRA sects 5 & 8

301 Take extra care where the track crosses from one side of the road to the other and where the road narrows and the tracks come close to the kerb. Tram drivers usually have their own traffic signals and may be permitted to move when you are not. Always give way to trams. Do not try to race or overtake them or pass them on the inside, unless they are at tram stops or stopped by tram signals and there is a designated tram lane for you to pass.

302 You **MUST NOT** park your vehicle where it would get in the way of trams or where it would force other drivers to do so. Do not stop on any part of a tram track, except in a designated bay where this has been provided alongside and clear of the track. When doing so, ensure that all parts of your vehicle are outside the delineated tram path. Remember that a tram cannot steer round an obstruction.

Law RTRA sects 5 & 8

303 **Tram stops.** Where the tram stops at a platform, either in the middle or at the side of the road, you **MUST** follow the route shown by the road signs and markings. At stops without platforms you **MUST NOT** drive between a tram and the left-hand kerb when a tram has stopped to pick up passengers. If there is no alternative route signed, do not overtake the tram – wait until it moves off.

Law RTRA sects 5 & 8

304 Look out for pedestrians, especially children, running to catch a tram approaching a stop.

305 Always give priority to trams, especially when they signal to pull away from stops, unless it would be unsafe to do so. Remember that they may be carrying large numbers of standing passengers who could be injured if the tram had to make an emergency stop. Look out for people getting off a bus or tram and crossing the road.

306 All road users, but particularly cyclists and motorcyclists, should take extra care when driving or riding close to or crossing the tracks, especially if the rails are wet. You should take particular care when crossing the rails at shallow angles, on bends and at junctions. It is safest to cross the tracks directly at right angles. Other road users should be aware that cyclists and motorcyclists may need more space to cross the tracks safely.

307 **Overhead electric lines.** Tramway overhead wires are normally 5.8 metres above any carriageway, but can be lower. You should ensure that you have sufficient clearance between the wire and your vehicle (including any load you are carrying) before driving under an overhead wire. Drivers of vehicles with extending cranes, booms, tipping apparatus or other types of variable height equipment should ensure that the equipment is fully lowered. Where overhead wires are set lower than 5.8 metres, these will be indicated by height clearance markings – similar to 'low bridge' signs. The height clearances on these plates should be carefully noted and observed. If you are in any doubt as to whether your vehicle will pass safely under the wires, you should always contact the local police or the tramway operator. Never take a chance as this can be extremely hazardous.

Light signals controlling traffic

Traffic Light Signals

RED means 'Stop'. Wait behind the stop line on the carriageway

RED AND AMBER also means 'Stop'. Do not pass through or start until GREEN shows

GREEN means you may go on if the way is clear. Take special care if you intend to turn left or right and give way to pedestrians who are crossing

AMBER means 'Stop' at the stop line. You may go on only if the AMBER appears after you have crossed the stop line or are so close to it that to pull up might cause an accident

A GREEN ARROW may be provided in addition to the full green signal if movement in a certain direction is allowed before or after the full green phase. If the way is clear you may go but only in the direction shown by the arrow. You may do this whatever other lights may be showing. White light signals may be provided for trams

Flashing red lights

Alternately flashing red lights mean YOU MUST STOP

At level crossings, lifting bridges, airfields, fire stations, etc.

Motorway signals

You **MUST NOT** proceed further in this lane

Change lane

Reduced visibility ahead

Lane ahead closed

    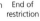

Temporary maximum speed advised and information message

Leave motorway at next exit

Temporary maximum speed advised

End of restriction

Lane control signals

Green arrow – lane available to traffic facing the sign
Red crosses – lane closed to traffic facing the sign
White diagonal arrow – change lanes in direction shown

Direction indicator signals

I intend to move out to
the right or turn right

I intend to move in to the left
or turn left or stop on the left

Brake light signals

I am applying the brakes

Reversing light signals

I intend to reverse

These signals should not be used except for the purposes described.

Arm signals

For use when direction indicator signals are not used, or when necessary to reinforce direction indicator signals and stop lights. **Also for use by pedal cyclists and those in charge of horses.**

I intend to move in to
the left or turn left

I intend to move out to
the right or turn right

I intend to slow down
or stop

Signals by authorised persons

Police officers

Stop

Traffic approaching from the front

Traffic approaching from both front and behind

Traffic approaching from behind

To beckon traffic on

From the side

From the front

From behind*

Arm signals to persons controlling traffic

I want to go straight on

I want to turn left; use either hand

I want to turn right

* In Wales, bilingual signs appear on emergency services vehicles and clothing

Vehicle and Operator Services Agency and Highways Agency Traffic Officers

Highways Agency Traffic Officer

VOSA Traffic Officer

These officers now have new powers to stop/direct vehicles and will be using hand signals and light signals similar to those used by police.
You **MUST** obey any signals given (see Rules 107 and 108).

School Crossing Patrols

Not ready to cross pedestrians

Barrier to stop pedestrians crossing

Ready to cross pedestrians, vehicles must be prepared to stop

All vehicles must stop

Signs giving orders

Signs with red circles are mostly prohibitive.

Plates below signs qualify their message.

Entry to
20 mph zone

End of
20 mph zone

Maximum
speed

National speed
limit applies

School crossing
patrol

Stop and
give way

Give way to
traffic on
major road

Manually operated temporary
STOP and GO signs

No entry for
vehicular traffic

No vehicles
except bicycles
being pushed

No cycling

No motor
vehicles

No buses
(over 8
passenger
seats)

No
overtaking

No
towed
caravans

No vehicles
carrying
explosives

No vehicle or
combination of
vehicles over
length shown

No vehicles
over
height shown

No vehicles
over
width shown

Give priority to vehicles
from opposite direction

No right turn

No left turn

No
U-turns

No goods vehicles over
maximum gross weight
shown (in tonnes) except for
loading and unloading

Note: Although *The Highway Code* shows many of the signs commonly in use, a comprehensive explanation of our signing system is given in the Department's booklet *Know Your Traffic Signs*, which is on sale at booksellers. The booklet also illustrates and explains the vast majority of signs the road user is likely to encounter. The signs illustrated in *The Highway Code* are not all drawn to the same scale. In Wales, bilingual versions of some signs are used including Welsh and English versions of place names. Some older designs of signs may still be seen on the roads.

No vehicles over maximum gross weight shown (in tonnes)

Parking restricted to permit holders

No stopping during period indicated except for buses

No stopping during times shown except for as long as necessary to set down or pick up passengers

No waiting

No stopping (Clearway)

Signs with blue circles but no red border mostly give positive instruction.

Ahead only

Turn left ahead (right if symbol reversed)

Turn left (right if symbol reversed)

Keep left (right if symbol reversed)

Vehicles may pass either side to reach same destination

Mini-roundabout (roundabout circulation – give way to vehicles from the immediate right)

Route to be used by pedal cycles only

Segregated pedal cycle and pedestrian route

Minimum speed

End of minimum speed

Buses and cycles only

Trams only

Pedestrian crossing point over tramway

One-way traffic (note: compare circular 'Ahead only' sign)

With-flow bus and cycle lane

Contra-flow bus lane

With-flow pedal cycle lane

Warning signs

Mostly triangular

Dual carriageway ends

Road narrows on right (left if symbol reversed)

Road narrows on both sides

Distance to 'STOP' line ahead

Distance to 'Give Way' line ahead

Crossroads

Junction on bend ahead

T-junction with priority over vehicles from the right

Staggered junction

Traffic merging from left ahead

The priority through route is indicated by the broader line.

Double bend first to left (symbol may be reversed)

Bend to right (or left if symbol reversed)

Roundabout

Uneven road

Plate below some signs

Two-way traffic crosses one-way road

Two-way traffic straight ahead

Opening or swing bridge ahead

Low-flying aircraft or sudden aircraft noise

Falling or fallen rocks

Traffic signals not in use

Traffic signals

Slippery road

Steep hill downwards

Steep hill upwards

Gradients may be shown as a ratio
i.e. 20% = 1:5

Tunnel ahead

Trams crossing ahead

Level crossing with barrier or gate ahead

Level crossing without barrier or gate ahead

Level crossing without barrier

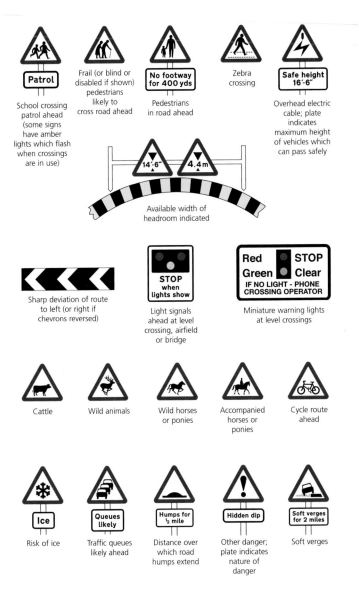

School crossing patrol ahead (some signs have amber lights which flash when crossings are in use)

Frail (or blind or disabled if shown) pedestrians likely to cross road ahead

Pedestrians in road ahead

Zebra crossing

Overhead electric cable; plate indicates maximum height of vehicles which can pass safely

Available width of headroom indicated

Sharp deviation of route to left (or right if chevrons reversed)

Light signals ahead at level crossing, airfield or bridge

Miniature warning lights at level crossings

Cattle

Wild animals

Wild horses or ponies

Accompanied horses or ponies

Cycle route ahead

Risk of ice

Traffic queues likely ahead

Distance over which road humps extend

Other danger; plate indicates nature of danger

Soft verges

Side winds

Hump bridge

Worded warning sign

Quayside or river bank

Risk of grounding

Direction signs

Mostly rectangular

Signs on motorways – blue backgrounds

At a junction leading directly into a motorway (junction number may be shown on a black background)

On approaches to junctions (junction number on black background)

Route confirmatory sign after junction

Downward pointing arrows mean 'Get in lane'
The left-hand lane leads to a different destination from the other lanes.

The panel with the inclined arrow indicates the destinations which can be reached by leaving the motorway at the next junction

Signs on primary routes – green backgrounds

On approaches to junctions

At the junction

Route confirmatory sign after junction

On approaches to junctions

On approach to a junction in Wales (bilingual)

Blue panels indicate that the motorway starts at the junction ahead.
Motorways shown in brackets can also be reached along the route indicated.
White panels indicate local or non-primary routes leading from the junction ahead.
Brown panels show the route to tourist attractions.
The name of the junction may be shown at the top of the sign.
The aircraft symbol indicates the route to an airport.
A symbol may be included to warn of a hazard or restriction along that route.

Green background signs – continued

Primary route forming
part of a ring road

Signs on non-primary and local routes – black borders

On approaches to junctions

Market
Walborough 7
B 486

At the junction

Direction to toilets
with access for the
disabled

Green panels indicate that the primary route starts at the junction ahead.
Route numbers on a blue background show the direction to a motorway.
Route numbers on a green background show the direction to a primary route.

Other direction signs

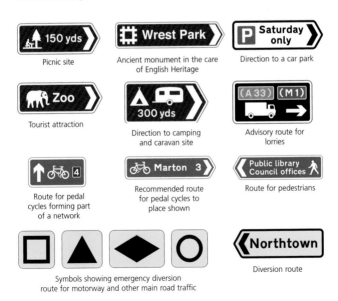

150 yds — Picnic site

Wrest Park — Ancient monument in the care of English Heritage

Saturday only — Direction to a car park

Zoo — Tourist attraction

300 yds — Direction to camping and caravan site

(A33) (M1) — Advisory route for lorries

Route for pedal cycles forming part of a network

Marton 3 — Recommended route for pedal cycles to place shown

Public library
Council offices — Route for pedestrians

Symbols showing emergency diversion route for motorway and other main road traffic

Northtown — Diversion route

Information signs

All rectangular

Entrance to controlled parking zone

Entrance to congestion charging zone

End of controlled parking zone

Advance warning of restriction or prohibition ahead

Parking place for solo motorcycles

With-flow bus lane ahead which pedal cycles and taxis may also use

Lane designated for use by high occupancy vehicles (HOV) – see rule 142

Vehicles permitted to use an HOV lane ahead

End of motorway

Start of motorway and point from which motorway regulations apply

Appropriate traffic lanes at junction ahead

Traffic on the main carriageway coming from right has priority over joining traffic

Additional traffic joining from left ahead. Traffic on main carriageway has priority over joining traffic from right-hand lane of slip road

Traffic in right-hand lane of slip road joining the main carriageway has prority over left-hand lane

'Countdown' markers at exit from motorway (each bar represents 100 yards to the exit). Green-backed markers may be used on primary routes and white-backed markers with black bars on other routes. At approaches to concealed level crossings white-backed markers with red bars may be used. Although these will be erected at equal distances the bars do not represent 100 yard intervals.

Motorway service area sign showing the operator's name

Information signs – continued

Traffic has priority
over oncoming
vehicles

Hospital ahead with
Accident and
Emergency facilities

Tourist
information
point

No through road
for vehicles

Recommended
route for pedal
cycles

Home Zone Entry

Area in which
cameras are
used to enforce
traffic regulations

Bus lane on road at
junction ahead

Road works signs

Road works

Loose
chippings

Temporary hazard
at road works

Temporary lane closure
(the number and position
of arrows and red bars
may be varied according
to lanes open and closed)

Slow-moving or
stationary works
vehicle blocking a
traffic lane. Pass in
the direction shown
by the arrow.

Mandatory
speed
limit ahead

Road works
1 mile ahead

End of road works and
any temporary restrictions
including speed limits

Signs used on the back of slow-moving or
stationary vehicles warning of a lane closed
ahead by a works vehicle. There are no
cones on the road.

Lane restrictions at
road works ahead

One lane crossover
at contraflow
road works

Across the carriageway

Stop line at signals or police control

Stop line at 'Stop' sign

Stop line for pedestrians at a level crossing

Give way to traffic on major road (can also be used at mini roundabouts)

Give way to traffic from the right at a roundabout

Give way to traffic from the right at a mini-roundabout

Along the carriageway

Edge line

Centre line
See Rule 127

Hazard warning line
See Rule 127

Double white lines
See Rules 128 and 129

See Rule 130

Lane line See Rule 131

Along the edge of the carriageway

Waiting restrictions

Waiting restrictions indicated by yellow lines apply to the carriageway, pavement and verge. You may stop to load or unload (unless there are also loading restrictions as described below) or while passengers board or alight. Double yellow lines mean no waiting at any time, unless there are signs that specifically indicate seasonal restrictions. The times at which the restrictions apply for other road markings are shown on nearby plates or on entry signs to controlled parking zones. If no days are shown on the signs, the restrictions are in force every day including Sundays and Bank Holidays. White bay markings and upright signs (see below) indicate where parking is allowed.

No waiting
at any time

No waiting
during times
shown on sign

Waiting is limited to the
duration specified during the
days and times shown

Red Route stopping controls

Red lines are used on some roads instead of yellow lines. In London the double and single red lines used on Red Routes indicate that stopping to park, load/unload or to board and alight from a vehicle (except for a licensed taxi or if you hold a Blue Badge) is prohibited. The red lines apply to the carriageway, pavement and verge. The times that the red line prohibitions apply are shown on nearby signs, but the double red line ALWAYS means no stopping at any time. On Red Routes you may stop to park, load/unload in specially marked boxes and adjacent signs specify the times and purposes and duration allowed. A box MARKED IN RED indicates that it may only be available for the purpose specified for part of the day (eg between busy peak periods). A box MARKED IN WHITE means that it is available throughout the day.

RED AND SINGLE YELLOW LINES CAN ONLY GIVE A GUIDE TO THE RESTRICTIONS AND CONTROLS IN FORCE AND SIGNS, NEARBY OR AT A ZONE ENTRY, MUST BE CONSULTED.

No stopping
at any time

No stopping
during times
shown on sign

Parking is limited to the
duration specified during
the days and times
shown

Only loading may take
place at the times shown
for up to a maximum
duration of 20 mins

On the kerb or at the edge of the carriageway

Loading restrictions on roads other than Red Routes

Yellow marks on the kerb or at the edge of the carriageway indicate that loading or unloading is prohibited at the times shown on the nearby black and white plates. You may stop while passengers board or alight. If no days are indicated on the signs the restrictions are in force every day including Sundays and Bank Holidays.

ALWAYS CHECK THE TIMES SHOWN ON THE PLATES.

Lengths of road reserved for vehicles loading and unloading are indicated by a white 'bay' marking with the words 'Loading Only' and a sign with the white on blue 'trolley' symbol. This sign also shows whether loading and unloading is restricted to goods vehicles and the times at which the bay can be used. If no times or days are shown it may be used at any time. Vehicles may not park here if they are not loading or unloading.

No loading or
unloading
at any time

No loading or
unloading
at the times shown

Loading bay

Other road markings

Keep entrance clear of stationary vehicles, even if picking up or setting down children

Warning of 'Give Way'
just ahead

Parking space reserved
for vehicles named

See Rule 243

See Rule 141

Box junction – See
Rule 174

Do not block that part of
the carriageway indicated

Indication of traffic
lanes

Large goods vehicle rear markings

Motor vehicles over 7500 kilograms maximum gross weight and trailers over 3500 kilograms maximum gross weight

Left

Right

Central

The vertical markings are also required to be fitted to builders' skips placed in the road, commercial vehicles or combinations longer than 13 metres (optional on combinations between 11 and 13 metres)

Hazard warning plates

Certain tank vehicles carrying dangerous goods must display hazard information panels

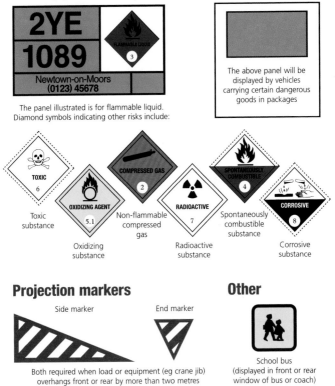

2YE
1089
Newtown-on-Moors
(0123) 45678

FLAMMABLE LIQUID
3

The panel illustrated is for flammable liquid. Diamond symbols indicating other risks include:

The above panel will be displayed by vehicles carrying certain dangerous goods in packages

TOXIC
6

Toxic substance

OXIDIZING AGENT
5.1

Oxidizing substance

COMPRESSED GAS
2

Non-flammable compressed gas

RADIOACTIVE
7

Radioactive substance

SPONTANEOUSLY COMBUSTIBLE
4

Spontaneously combustible substance

CORROSIVE
8

Corrosive substance

Projection markers

Side marker

End marker

Both required when load or equipment (eg crane jib) overhangs front or rear by more than two metres

Other

School bus (displayed in front or rear window of bus or coach)

111

1. You and your bicycle

Make sure that you feel confident of your ability to ride safely on the road. Be sure that

- you choose the right size and type of cycle for comfort and safety
- lights and reflectors are kept clean and in good working order
- tyres are in good condition and inflated to the pressure shown on the tyre
- gears are working correctly
- the chain is properly adjusted and oiled
- the saddle and handlebars are adjusted to the correct height.

It is recommended that you fit a bell to your cycle.

You **MUST**

- ensure your brakes are efficient
- at night, use lit front and rear lights and have a red rear reflector.

Laws PCUR regs 6 & 10 & RVLR reg 18

Cycle training can help both children and adults, especially those adults returning to cycling to develop the skills needed to cycle safely on today's roads. A new national cycle training standard has been developed which the Government is promoting and making funding available for delivery in schools.

All cyclists should consider the benefits of undertaking cycle training. For information, contact your local authority.

2. Motorcycle licence requirements

If you have a provisional motorcycle licence, you **MUST** satisfactorily complete a Compulsory Basic Training (CBT) course. You can then ride on the public road, with L plates (in Wales either D plates, L plates or both can be used), for up to two years. To obtain your full motorcycle licence you **MUST** pass a motorcycle theory test and then a practical test.

Law MV(DL)R regs 16 & 68

If you have a full car licence you may ride motorcycles up to 125 cc and 11 kW power output, with L plates (and/or D plates in Wales), on public roads, but you **MUST** first satisfactorily complete a CBT course if you have not already done so.

Law MV(DL)R reg 43

If you have a full moped licence and wish to obtain full motorcycle entitlement, you will be required to take a motorcycle theory test if you did not take a separate theory test when you obtained your moped licence. You **MUST** then pass a practical motorcycle test. Note that if CBT was completed for the full moped licence there is no need to repeat it, but if the moped test was taken before 1/12/90 CBT will need to be completed before riding a motorcycle as a learner.

Law MV(DL)R regs 42(1) & 69(1)

Light motorcycle licence (A1): you take a test on a motorcycle of between 75 and 125 cc. If you pass you may ride a motorcycle up to 125 cc with power output up to 11 kW.

Standard motorcycle licence (A): if your test vehicle is between 120 and 125 cc and capable of more than 100 km/h you will be given a standard (A) licence. You will then be restricted to motorcycles of up to 25 kW for two years. After two years you may ride any size machine.

Direct or Accelerated Access enables riders over the age of 21, or those who reach 21 before their two-year restriction ends, to ride larger motorcycles sooner. To obtain a licence to do so they are required to

- have successfully completed a CBT course
- pass a theory test, if they are required to do so
- pass a practical test on a machine with power output of at least 35 kW.

To practise, they can ride larger motorcycles, with L plates (and/or D plates in Wales), on public roads, but only when accompanied by an approved instructor on another motorcycle in radio contact.

You **MUST NOT** carry a pillion passenger or pull a trailer until you have passed your test.

Law MV(DL)R reg 16

Moped licence requirements

A moped **MUST** have an engine capacity not exceeding 50 cc, not weigh more than 250 kg and be designed to have a maximum speed not exceeding 31 mph (50 km/h). From June 2003 all EC Type Approved mopeds have been restricted to 28 mph (45 km/h).

Law RTA 1988 (as amended) sect 108

To ride a moped, learners **MUST**

- ➲ be 16 or over
- ➲ have a provisional moped licence
- ➲ complete CBT training.

You **MUST** first pass the theory test for motorcycles and then the moped practical test to obtain your full moped licence. If you passed your driving test before 1 February 2001 you are qualified to ride a moped without L plates (and/or D plates in Wales), although it is recommended that you complete CBT before riding on the road. If you passed your driving test after this date you **MUST** complete CBT before riding a moped on the road.

Laws RTA 1988 sects 97(e) & 101 & MV(DL)R regs 38(4) & 43

Note. For motorcycle and moped riders wishing to upgrade, the following give exemption from taking the motorcycle theory test

- ➲ full A1 motorcycle licence
- ➲ full moped licence, if gained after 1/7/96.

Law MV(DL)R reg 42

3. Motor vehicle documentation and learner driver requirements

Documents

Driving licence. You **MUST** have a valid driving licence for the category of motor vehicle you are driving. You **MUST** inform the Driver and Vehicle Licensing Agency (DVLA) if you change your name and/or address.

Law RTA 1988 sects 87 & 99(4)

Holders of non-European Community licences who are now resident in the UK may only drive on that licence for a maximum of 12 months from the date they become resident in this country.

To ensure continuous driving entitlement

⤴ a British provisional licence should be obtained and
a driving test(s) passed before the 12-month period
elapses, or

⤴ in the case of a driver who holds a licence from a country
which has been designated in law for licence exchange
purposes, the driver should exchange the licence for
a British one.

MOT. Cars and motorcycles **MUST** normally pass an MOT
test three years from the date of the first registration
and every year after that. You **MUST NOT** drive a motor
vehicle without an MOT certificate when it should have
one. Exceptionally, you may drive to a pre-arranged test
appointment or to a garage for repairs required for the
test. Driving an unroadworthy motor vehicle may invalidate
your insurance.
Law RTA 1988 sects 45, 47, 49 & 53

Insurance. To use a motor vehicle on the road, you **MUST**
have a valid insurance policy. This **MUST** at least cover you
for injury or damage to a third party while using that motor
vehicle. Before driving any motor vehicle, make sure that
it has this cover for your use or that your own insurance
provides adequate cover. You **MUST NOT** drive a motor
vehicle without insurance. Also, be aware that even if
a road traffic incident is not your fault, you may still be
held liable by insurance companies.
Law RTA 1988 sect 143

Uninsured drivers can now be automatically detected by
roadside cameras. Further to the penalties for uninsured
driving listed on page 120, an offender's vehicle can now
be seized by the Police, taken away and crushed.
Law RTA 1988, sects 165a & 165b

The types of cover available are indicated below:

Third-Party insurance – this is often the cheapest form
of insurance, and is the minimum cover required by law.
It covers anyone you might injure or whose property you
might damage. It does not cover damage to your own
motor vehicle or injury to yourself.

Third-Party, Fire and Theft insurance – similar to
third-party, but also covers you against your motor
vehicle being stolen, or damaged by fire.

Comprehensive insurance – this is the most expensive but the best insurance. Apart from covering other persons and property against injury or damage, it also covers damage to your own motor vehicle, up to the market value of that vehicle, and personal injury to yourself.

Registration certificate. Registration certificates (also called harmonised registration certificates) are issued for all motor vehicles used on the road, describing them (make, model, etc) and giving details of the registered keeper. You **MUST** notify the Driver and Vehicle Licensing Agency in Swansea as soon as possible when you buy or sell a motor vehicle, or if you change your name or address. For registration certificates issued after 27 March 1997, the buyer and seller are responsible for completing the registration certificates. The seller is responsible for forwarding them to DVLA. The procedures are explained on the back of the registration certificates.
Law RV(R&L)R regs 21, 22, 23 & 24

Vehicle Excise Duty (VED). All motor vehicles used or kept on public roads **MUST** display a valid Vehicle Excise Duty disc (tax disc) displayed at all times. Even motor vehicles exempt from duty **MUST** display a tax disc at all times.
Law VERA sects 29 and 33

Statutory Off-Road Notification (SORN). This is a notification to the DVLA that a motor vehicle is not being used on the road. If you are the vehicle keeper and want to keep a motor vehicle untaxed and off the public road you **MUST** declare SORN – it is an offence not to do so. You then won't have to pay any road tax for that vehicle for a period of 12 months. You need to send a further declaration after that period if the vehicle is still off the public road. The SORN will end if you sell the vehicle and the new owner will become immediately responsible.
Law RV(RL)R 2002, reg 26 sched 4

Production of documents. You **MUST** be able to produce your driving licence and counterpart, a valid insurance certificate and (if appropriate) a valid MOT certificate, when requested by a police officer. If you cannot do this you may be asked to take them to a police station within seven days.
Law RTA 1988 sects 164 & 165

Learner drivers

Learners driving a car **MUST** hold a valid provisional licence.
They **MUST** be supervised by someone at least 21 years old
who holds a full EC/EEA licence for that type of car (automatic
or manual) and has held one for at least three years.

Laws MV(DL)R reg 16 & RTA 1988 sect 87

Vehicles. Any vehicle driven by a learner **MUST** display red
L plates. In Wales, either red D plates, red L plates, or both,
can be used. Plates **MUST** conform to legal specifications
and **MUST** be clearly visible to others from in front of the
vehicle and from behind. Plates should be removed or
covered when not being driven by a learner (except on
driving school vehicles).

Law MV(DL)R reg 16 & sched 4

You **MUST** pass the theory test (if one is required) and
then a practical driving test for the category of vehicle you
wish to drive before driving unaccompanied.

Law MV(DL)R reg 40

4. The road user and the law

Road traffic law

The following list can be found abbreviated throughout the
Code. It is not intended to be a comprehensive guide, but a
guide to some of the important points of law. For the precise
wording of the law, please refer to the various Acts and
Regulations (as amended) indicated in the Code.
Abbreviations are listed on the following page.

Most of the provisions apply on all roads throughout Great
Britain, although there are some exceptions. The definition
of a road in England and Wales is 'any highway and any
other road to which the public has access and includes
bridges over which a road passes' (RTA 1988 sect 192(1)).
In Scotland, there is a similar definition which is extended
to include any way over which the public have a right of
passage (R(S)A 1984 sect 151(1)).

It is important to note that references to 'road' therefore
generally include footpaths, bridleways and cycle tracks, and
many roadways and driveways on private land (including many
car parks). In most cases, the law will apply to them and there
may be additional rules for particular paths or ways. Some
serious driving offences, including drink-driving offences, also
apply to all public places, for example public car parks.

Chronically Sick & Disabled Persons Act 1970	CSDPA
Functions of Traffic Wardens Order 1970	FTWO
Greater London (General Powers) Act 1974	GL(GP)A
Highway Act 1835 or 1980 (as indicated)	HA
Horses (Protective Headgear for Young Riders) Act 1990	H(PHYR)A
Horses (Protective Headgear for Young Riders) Regulations 1992	H(PHYR)R
Motor Cycles (Eye Protectors) Regulations 1999	MC(EP)R
Motor Cycles (Protective Helmets) Regulations 1998	MC(PH)R
Motorways Traffic (England & Wales) Regulations 1982	MT(E&W)R
Motorways Traffic (England & Wales) Amended Regulations	MT(E&W)(A)R
Motorways Traffic (Scotland) Regulations 1995	MT(S)R
Motor Vehicles (Driving Licences) Regulations 1999	MV(DL)R
Motor Vehicles (Wearing of Seat Belts) Regulations 1993	MV(WSB)R
Motor Vehicles (Wearing of Seat Belts) (Amendment) Regulations 2006	MV(WSB)(A)R
Motor Vehicles (Wearing of Seat Belts by Children in Front Seats) Regulations 1993	MV(WSBCFS)R
New Roads and Streetworks Act 1991	NRSWA
Pedal Cycles (Construction & Use) Regulations 1983	PCUR
Powers of Criminal Courts (Sentencing) Act 2000	PCC(S)A
Police Reform Act 2002	PRA
Prohibition of Smoking in Certain Premises (Scotland) Regulations 2006. Scottish SI 2006/No 90	TPSCP(S)R*
Public Passenger Vehicles Act 1981	PPVA
Road Safety Act 2006	RSA
Road Traffic Act 1984, 1988 or 1991 (as indicated)	RTA
Road Traffic (New Drivers) Act 1995	RT(ND)A
Road Traffic Offenders Act 1988	RTOA
Road Traffic Regulation Act 1984	RTRA
Road Vehicles (Construction & Use) Regulations 1986	CUR
Road Vehicles (Display of Registration Marks) Regulations 2001	RV(DRM)R
Road Vehicles Lighting Regulations 1989	RVLR
Road Vehicles (Registration & Licensing) Regulations 2002	RV(R&L)R
Roads (Scotland) Act 1984	R(S)A
Smoke-free (Exemptions and Vehicles) Regulations 2007 SI 2007/765	TSf(EV)*
Smoke-free Premises etc (Wales) Regulations 2007 SI 2007/W787	TSfP(W)R*
Traffic Management Act 2004	TMA
Traffic Signs Regulations & General Directions 2002	TSRGD
Use of Invalid Carriages on Highways Regulations 1988	UICHR
Vehicle Excise and Registration Act 1994	VERA
Zebra, Pelican and Puffin Pedestrian Crossings Regulations and General Directions 1997	ZPPPCRGD

Acts and regulations from 1988 can be viewed on the Office of Public Sector Information website (www.opsi.gov.uk). Acts and regulations prior to 1988 are only available in their original print format which may be obtained from The Stationery Office as detailed inside the back cover.

*Specific legislation applies to smoking in vehicles which constitute workplaces. For information, visit
www.smokefreeengland.co.uk
www.clearingtheairscotland.com
www.smokingbanwales.co.uk

5. Penalties

Parliament sets the maximum penalties for road traffic offences. The seriousness of the offence is reflected in the maximum penalty. It is for the courts to decide what sentence to impose according to circumstances.

The penalty table on page 120 indicates some of the main offences, and the associated penalties. There is a wide range of other more specific offences which, for the sake of simplicity, are not shown here. The penalty points and disqualification system is described below.

Penalty points and disqualification

The penalty point system is intended to deter drivers and motorcyclists from following unsafe motoring practices. Certain non-motoring offences, e.g. failure to rectify vehicle defects, can also attract penalty points. The court **MUST** order points to be endorsed on the licence according to the fixed number or the range set by Parliament. The accumulation of penalty points acts as a warning to drivers and motorcyclists that they risk disqualification if further offences are committed.

Law RTOA sects 44 & 45

A driver or motorcyclist who accumulates 12 or more penalty points within a three-year period **MUST** be disqualified. This will be for a minimum period of six months, or longer if the driver or motorcyclist has previously been disqualified.

Law RTOA sect 35

For every offence which carries penalty points the court has a discretionary power to order the licence holder to be disqualified. This may be for any period the court thinks fit, but will usually be between a week and a few months.

In the case of serious offences, such as dangerous driving and drink-driving, the court **MUST** order disqualification. The minimum period is 12 months, but for repeat offenders or where the alcohol level is high, it may be longer. For example, a second drink-drive offence in the space of 10 years will result in a minimum of three years' disqualification.

Law RTOA sect 34

Penalty Table

Offence	Imprisonment	Maximum Penalties Fine	Disqualification	Penalty Points
*causing death by dangerous driving	14 years	Unlimited	Obligatory – 2 years minimum	3–11 (if exceptionally not disqualified)
*Dangerous driving	2 years	Unlimited	Obligatory	3–11 (if exceptionally not disqualified)
*Causing death by careless driving under the influence of drink or drugs	14 years	Unlimited	Obligatory – 2 years minimum	3–11 (if exceptionally not disqualified)
Careless and inconsiderate driving	-	£5,000	Discretionary	3–9
Driving while unfit through drink or drugs or with excess alcohol: or failing to provide a specimen for analysis	6 months	£5,000	Obligatory	3–11 (if exceptionally not disqualified)
Failing to stop after an accident or failing to report an accident	6 months	£5,000	Discretionary	5–10
Driving when disqualified	6 months (12 months in Scotland)	£5,000	Discretionary	6
Driving after refusal or revocation of licence on medical grounds	6 months	£5,000	Discretionary	3–6
Driving without insurance	-	£5,000	Discretionary	6–8
Using a vehicle in a dangerous condition	-	LGV £5,000 PCV £5,000 Other £2,500	Obligatory if offence committed within 3 years of a previous conviction for the same offence – 6 months min otherwise discretionary	3 in each case
Failure to have proper control of vehicle or full view of the road and traffic ahead, or using a hand-held mobile phone while driving	-	£1,000 (£2,500 for PCV or goods vehicle)	Discretionary	3
Driving otherwise than in accordance with a licence	-	£1,000	Discretionary	3–6
Speeding	-	£1,000 (£2,500 for motorway offences)	Discretionary	3–6 or 3 (fixed penalty)
Traffic light offences	-	£1,000	Discretionary	3
No MOT certificate	-	£1,000	-	-
Seat belt offences	-	£500	-	-
Dangerous cycling	-	£2,500	-	-
Careless cycling	-	£1,000	-	-
Cycling on pavement	-	£500	-	-
Failing to identify driver of a vehicle	-	£1,000	Discretionary	6

*Where a court disqualifies a person on conviction for one of these offences, it must order an extended retest. The courts also have discretion to order a retest for any other offence which carries penalty points, an extended retest where disqualification is obligatory, and an ordinary test where disqualification is not obligatory.

Furthermore, in some serious cases, the court **MUST** (in addition to imposing a fixed period of disqualification) order the offender to be disqualified until they pass a driving test. In other cases the court has a discretionary power to order such disqualification. The test may be an ordinary length test or an extended test according to the nature of the offence.

Law RTOA sect 36

New drivers. Special rules as set out below apply for a period of two years from the date of passing their first driving test, to drivers and motorcyclists from

- the UK, EU/EEA, the Isle of Man, the Channel Islands or Gibraltar who passed their first driving test in any of those countries
- other foreign countries who have to pass a UK driving test to gain a UK licence, in which case the UK driving test is treated as their first driving test; and
- other foreign countries who (without needing a test) exchanged their licence for a UK licence and subsequently passed a UK driving test to drive another type of vehicle, in which case the UK driving test is treated as their first driving test. For example a driver who exchanges a foreign licence (car) for a UK licence (car) and who later passes a test to drive another type of vehicle (e.g. an HGV) will be subject to the special rules.

Where a person subject to the special rules accumulates six or more penalty points before the end of the two-year period (including any points acquired before passing the test) their licence will be revoked automatically. To regain the licence they must reapply for a provisional licence and may drive only as a learner until they pass a further driving test (also see Annex 8 – Safety code for new drivers.)

Law RT(ND)A

Note. This applies even if they pay for offences by fixed penalty. Drivers in the first group (UK, EU/EEA etc.) who already have a full licence for one type of vehicle are not affected by the special rules if they later pass a test to drive another type of vehicle.

Other consequences of offending

Where an offence is punishable by imprisonment then the vehicle used to commit the offence may be confiscated.

Law PCC(S)A, sect 143

In addition to the penalties a court may decide to impose, the cost of insurance is likely to rise considerably following conviction for a serious driving offence. This is because insurance companies consider such drivers are more likely to be involved in a collision.

Drivers disqualified for drinking and driving twice within 10 years, or once if they are over two and a half times the legal limit, or those who refused to give a specimen, also have to satisfy the Driver and Vehicle Licensing Agency's Medical Branch that they do not have an alcohol problem and are otherwise fit to drive before their licence is returned at the end of their period of disqualification. Persistent misuse of drugs or alcohol may lead to the withdrawal of a driving licence.

6. Vehicle maintenance, safety and security

Vehicle maintenance
Take special care that lights, brakes, steering, exhaust system, seat belts, demisters, wipers and washers are all working. Also

- lights, indicators, reflectors, and number plates **MUST** be kept clean and clear
- windscreens and windows **MUST** be kept clean and free from obstructions to vision
- lights **MUST** be properly adjusted to prevent dazzling other road users. Extra attention needs to be paid to this if the vehicle is heavily loaded
- exhaust emissions **MUST NOT** exceed prescribed levels
- ensure your seat, seat belt, head restraint and mirrors are adjusted correctly before you drive
- ensure that items of luggage are securely stowed.

Laws RVLR 1989 regs 23 & 27 & CUR 1986, regs 30 & 61

Warning displays. Make sure that you understand the meaning of all warning displays on the vehicle instrument panel. Do not ignore warning signs, they could indicate a dangerous fault developing.

- When you turn the ignition key, warning lights will be illuminated but will go out when the engine starts (except the handbrake warning light). If they do not, or if they come on while you are driving, stop and investigate the problem, as you could have a serious fault.

↻ If the charge warning light comes on while you are driving, it may mean that the battery isn't charging. This should also be checked as soon as possible to avoid loss of power to lights and other electrical systems.

Window tints. You **MUST NOT** use a vehicle with excessively dark tinting applied to the windscreen, or to the glass in any front window to either side of the driver. Window tinting applied during manufacture complies with the Visual Light Transmittance (VLT) standards. There are no VLT limits for rear windscreens or rear passenger windows.

Laws RTA 1988 sect 42 & CUR reg 32

Tyres. Tyres MUST be correctly inflated to the vehicle manufacturer's specification for the load being carried. Always refer to the vehicle's handbook or data. Tyres should also be free from certain cuts and other defects.

Cars, light vans and light trailers **MUST** have a tread depth of at least 1.6 mm across the central three-quarters of the breadth of the tread and around the entire circumference.

Motorcycles, large vehicles and passenger-carrying vehicles **MUST** have a tread depth of at least 1 mm across three-quarters of the breadth of the tread and in a continuous band around the entire circumference.

Mopeds should have visible tread.

Be aware that some vehicle defects can attract penalty points.

Law CUR reg 27

If a tyre bursts while you are driving, try to keep control of your vehicle. Grip the steering wheel firmly and allow the vehicle to roll to a stop at the side of the road.

If you have a flat tyre, stop as soon as it is safe to do so. Only change the tyre if you can do so without putting yourself or others at risk – otherwise call a breakdown service.

Tyre pressures. Check weekly. Do this before your journey, when tyres are cold. Warm or hot tyres may give a misleading reading.

Your brakes and steering will be adversely affected by under-inflated or over-inflated tyres. Excessive or uneven tyre wear may be caused by faults in the braking or suspension systems, or wheels which are out of alignment. Have these faults corrected as soon as possible.

Fluid levels. Check the fluid levels in your vehicle at least weekly. Low brake fluid may result in brake failure and a crash. Make sure you recognise the low fluid warning lights if your vehicle has them fitted.

Before winter. Ensure that the battery is well maintained and that there are appropriate anti-freeze agents in your radiator and windscreen bottle.

Other problems. If your vehicle

- ⊃ pulls to one side when braking, it is most likely to be a brake fault or incorrectly inflated tyres. Consult a garage or mechanic immediately
- ⊃ continues to bounce after pushing down on the front or rear, its shock absorbers are worn. Worn shock absorbers can seriously affect the operation of a vehicle and should be replaced
- ⊃ smells of anything unusual such as burning rubber, petrol or an electrical fault; investigate immediately. Do not risk a fire.

Overheated engines or fire. Most engines are water-cooled. If your engine overheats you should wait until it has cooled naturally. Only then remove the coolant filler cap and add water or other coolant.

If your vehicle catches fire, get the occupants out of the vehicle quickly and to a safe place. Do not attempt to extinguish a fire in the engine compartment, as opening the bonnet will make the fire flare. Call the fire brigade.

Petrol stations/fuel tank/fuel leaks. Ensure that, when filling up your vehicle's tank or any fuel cans you are carrying, you do not spill fuel on the forecourt. Any spilled fuel should be immediately reported to the petrol station attendant. Diesel spillage is dangerous to other road users, particularly motorcyclists, as it will significantly reduce the level of grip between the tyres and road surface. Double-check for fuel leaks and make sure that

- ⊃ you do not overfill your fuel tank
- ⊃ the fuel cap is fastened securely
- ⊃ the seal in the cap is not torn, perished or missing
- ⊃ there is no visual damage to the cap or the fuel tank

Emergency fuel caps, if fitted, should form a good seal.

Never smoke, or use a mobile phone, on the forecourt of petrol stations as these are major fire risks and could cause an explosion.

Vehicle security
When you leave your vehicle you should

- ⟳ remove the ignition key and engage the steering lock
- ⟳ lock the car, even if you only leave it for a few minutes
- ⟳ close the windows completely
- ⟳ never leave children or pets in an unventilated car
- ⟳ take all contents with you, or lock them in the boot. Remember, for all a thief knows a carrier bag may contain valuables
- ⟳ never leave vehicle documents in the car.

For extra security fit an anti-theft device such as an alarm or immobiliser. If you are buying a new car it is a good idea to check the level of built-in security features. Consider having your registration number etched on all your car windows. This is a cheap and effective deterrent to professional thieves.

7. First Aid on the road

In the event of an incident, you can do a number of things to help, even if you have had no training.

1. Deal with danger
Further collisions and fire are the main dangers following a crash. Approach any vehicle involved with care. Switch off all engines and, if possible, warn other traffic. Stop anyone from smoking.

2. Get help
Try to get the assistance of bystanders. Get someone to call the appropriate emergency services as soon as possible. They will need to know the exact location of the incident and the number of vehicles involved.

3. Help those involved
DO NOT move casualties still in vehicles unless further danger is threatened. **DO NOT** remove a motorcyclist's helmet unless it is essential. Remember the casualty may be suffering from shock. **DO NOT** give them anything to eat or drink. **DO** try to make them warm and as comfortable as you can, but avoid unnecessary movement. **DO** give reassurance confidently and try not to leave them alone or let them wander into the path of other traffic.

4. Provide emergency care

Remember the letters **DR A B C**:

D – Danger – check that you are not in danger.
R – Response – try to get a response by asking questions and gently shaking their shoulders.
A – Airway – the airway should be clear and kept open. Place one hand on the forehead, two fingers under the chin and gently tilt the head back.
B – Breathing – normal breathing should be established. Once the airway is open check breathing for up to 10 seconds.
C – Compressions – if they are not breathing normally compressions should be administered to maintain circulation; place two hands in the centre of the chest and press down 4–5 cms at a rate of 100/minute. You may only need one hand for a child. Give 30 chest compressions. Then tilt the head back gently, pinch the casualty's nostrils together and place your mouth over theirs. Give two breaths, each lasting one second (use gentle breaths for a small child).

If the casualty is unconscious and breathing, place them in the recovery position until medical help arrives

Bleeding. First check for anything that may be in the wound, such as glass. If there is nothing embedded apply firm pressure over the wound. Take care not to press on the object – build up padding on either side of it. Fasten a pad to the wound with a bandage or length of cloth. Use the cleanest material available. If a limb is bleeding, but not broken, raise it above the level of the heart to reduce the flow of blood. Any restriction of blood circulation for more than a short time could cause long-term injuries.

Burns. Try to cool the burn by dousing it with clean, cold water or similar non-toxic liquid for at least 10 minutes. Do not try to remove anything sticking to the burn.

5. Be prepared

Always carry a first aid kit. You could save a life by learning emergency aid and first aid from a qualified organisation, such as the local ambulance services, the St John Ambulance Association and Brigade, St Andrew's Ambulance Association, the British Red Cross or any suitable qualified body (see page 129 for contact details).

8. Safety code for new drivers

Once you have passed the driving test you will be able to drive on your own. This will provide you with lots of opportunities but you need to remain safe. Even though you have shown you have the skills you need to drive safely, many newly qualified drivers lack experience. You need to continue to develop your skills, especially anticipating other road users' behaviour to avoid having a collision. As many as one new driver in five has some kind of collision in their first year of driving. This code provides advice to help you get through the first twelve months after passing the driving test, when you are most vulnerable, as safely as possible.

- Many of the worst collisions happen at night. Between midnight and 6 am is a time of high risk for new drivers. Avoid driving then unless it's really necessary.
- If you are driving with passengers, you are responsible for their safety. Don't let them distract you or encourage you to take risks. Tell your passengers that you need to concentrate if you are to get to your destination safely.
- Never show off or try to compete with other drivers, particularly if they are driving badly.
- Don't drive if you have consumed any alcohol or taken drugs. Even over-the-counter medicines can affect your ability to drive safely – read the label to see if they may affect your driving.
- Make sure everyone in the car is wearing a seat belt throughout the journey.
- Keep your speed down – many serious collisions happen because the driver loses control, particularly on bends.

⊃ Most new drivers have no experience of driving high-powered or sporty cars. Unless you have learnt to drive in such a vehicle you need to get plenty of experience driving on your own before driving a more powerful car.

⊃ Driving while uninsured is an offence. See Annex 3 for information on types of insurance cover.

REMEMBER that under the New Drivers Act you will have your licence revoked if you get six penalty points on your licence within two years of passing your first driving test. You will need to pass both the theory and practical tests again to get back your full licence.

You could consider taking further training such as Pass Plus, which could also save you money on your insurance, as well as helping you reduce your risk of being involved in a collision. There are three ways to find out more:

⊃ internet   – www.passplus.org.uk
⊃ telephone – DSA head office on 0115 901 2633
⊃ Email   – passplus@dsa.gsi.gov.uk

Other information

Metric conversions

The conversions given throughout *The Highway Code* are rounded but a detailed conversion chart is shown below.

Miles	Kilometres	Miles	Kilometres
1.00	1.61	40.00	64.37
5.00	8.05	45.00	72.42
10.00	16.09	50.00	80.47
15.00	24.14	55.00	88.51
20.00	32.19	60.00	96.56
25.00	40.23	65.00	104.60
30.00	48.28	70.00	112.65
35.00	56.33		

Useful websites

www.sja.org.uk   (St John Ambulance Association and Brigade)
www.firstaid.org.uk   (St Andrew's Ambulance Association)
www.redcross.org.uk   (The British Red Cross)
www.dft.gov.uk
www.direct.gov.uk
www.transportoffice.gov.uk
www.highways.gov.uk/traffic info
www.direct.gov.uk/highway code
www.larsoa.org.uk
www.collisionreporting.gov.uk
www.askthe.police.uk
www.parking-appeals.gov.uk (outside London)
www.parkingandtrafficappeals.gov.uk (inside London)

Further reading

Best practice

Further information about good driving and riding practice can be found in The Driving Standards Agency books *The Official DSA Guide to Driving – the essential skills* and *The Official DSA Guide to Riding – the essential skills*. Information specifically for drivers of large vehicles can be found in *The Official DSA Guide to Driving Goods Vehicles* and *The Official DSA Guide to Driving Buses and Coaches*.

The Blue Badge Scheme

Information on this scheme can be found on the Department for Transport Website: www.dft.gov.uk

Code of Practice for Horse-Drawn Vehicles

The Code of Practice is available from the Department for Transport, Transport Technology and Standards Division 6, 2nd Floor, Great Minster House, 76 Marsham Street, London SW1P 4DR.
Tel 0207 944 2078

Road works

A leaflet giving further information on driving through road works can be obtained from Highways Agency Publications, tel 0870 1226 236, quoting reference number HA113/04. For general Highways Agency information, tel 08457 504030 or email ha_info@highways.gsi.gov.uk

Caring for your car

Taking the time to look after your car makes a lot of sense. A well-maintained car is more economical and less likely to break down, and it will hold on to more of its value when you come to sell it. Doing simple maintenance jobs yourself will save you money too. Our guide shows you how.

Cleaning your car regularly helps protect it from damage and deterioration, and is vital to preserve your car's value when you come to sell it.

Washing a car

A car-wash is an easy option, but you can usually spot a car that's regularly been through a car-wash from the light scratches on its paintwork. Using a bucket and sponge to wash your car yourself will enable you to concentrate on any particularly dirty or tricky areas. You'll also be able to spot any stone chips or other damage, so that you can take action before they turn into bigger problems as rust takes hold. To get the best results when washing your car:

- Rinse the car first using cold water and a sponge to get rid of dirt and mud, and scrub the wheels. Thick mud can be soaked off using a hose.
- Always use a proper car shampoo, which will usually contain wax. Don't use washing-up liquid – it's much too harsh, and can damage the paint.
- Don't wash the car in bright sunlight, because the water will dry almost straight away, giving a blotchy finish.
- Take care not to put your sponge down on the ground, where it can pick up dirt and grit that could scratch the paintwork.
- When you've finished with the shampoo, rinse off with plenty of cold water, using a hose if possible. Dry off the bodywork using a soft chamois leather, which will absorb the water and give a shiny finish without streaks.

Polishing

If you find that the water no longer 'beads' on your car's paintwork when it rains or when you wash it, it's a good idea to apply a coat of polish.

Most modern polishes use wax and/or silicone, and these clean the paintwork and leave a layer of protective wax on top. Always wash the car, and dry it thoroughly, before polishing. Use two soft cloths – one for applying the polish, and one for buffing-off. Cotton cloths are best, as they avoid the problem of small particles of cloth sticking to the paint as you polish. Apply a thin, even layer of polish using a light circular motion, then let it dry to a haze (not a white powder), and lightly buff it off using your buffing cloth.

Wheels

To clean wheels, it's best to use a stiff-bristled (but not wire!) brush, and plenty of water. Brush the wheels thoroughly to remove the worst of the dirt before sponging. If your car has alloy wheels, using an alloy wheel cleaner and a brush should get rid of most of the dirt. Once you've got alloy wheels clean, polishing them makes dirt easier to remove in the future.

Interior

Fitting floor mats is a big help in keeping the interior of your car clean – they'll stop the worst of the dirt from marking the carpets, and they can simply be lifted out and brushed or washed off when cleaning the car.

Regular vacuuming also makes interior cleaning a lot easier. Don't forget to vacuum the boot and under the seats – it's surprising just how much dirt gets under the seats.

If you find any stains on the carpets, use a spray-on cleaner, working it in with a nail-brush and vacuuming or sponging off.

Check the seats for marks and use fabric cleaner to deal with these. Allow any dampened seats and carpets to dry before using the car. If you have access to a wet-and-dry vacuum cleaner this can be used to speed up the drying.

Plastic trim cleaner can revive tired or matt trim, and will also protect it against strong sunlight, which can cause fading.

Windows are best cleaned using a chamois leather, but difficult marks can be removed with a glass cleaner, buffing finally with a soft cloth. Over time the plastic trim in cars releases vapours into the air, causing a greasy film to build up on the interior glass – this is best removed with glass cleaner.

Washing a car regularly keeps it clean and helps protects its value too

Weekly checks

There are a few simple weekly checks that anyone can do. These checks only take about ten minutes and can help you to spot problems before they develop into serious trouble.

Checking the oil

Make sure the car is parked on level ground, with the engine stopped for at least five minutes, then find the oil level dipstick and pull it out of its tube.

Wipe the oil off the dipstick using a clean cloth, and look for the oil level markings on the bottom end of the dipstick. Push the dipstick slowly all the way back into its tube, then pull it out again and check the oil level. The level should be between the upper and lower marks. If the level is near the lower mark, you need to top up the oil.

To top up, remove the oil filler cap and pour in a little oil. A funnel will help to avoid spills. Wait a few seconds for the oil to drain down to the bottom of the engine, then re-check the oil level on the dipstick. If the level is still below the upper mark, repeat the topping-up procedure until the level reaches it. Don't overfill the engine with oil, as this can cause leaks and possibly damage.

When you've finished, refit the filler cap tightly, wipe away any spills, and make sure that the dipstick is pushed all the way back into its tube.

Checking the engine oil level on the dipstick is a quick and easy task

Top up the brake fluid reservoir with fresh fluid if it falls below the minimum

Brake fluid

With the car parked on level ground, find the brake fluid reservoir and check that the brake fluid level in the reservoir is up to the correct level, or between the 'MAX' and 'MIN' marks.

If the fluid needs topping up, slowly unscrew the cap from the reservoir. Many brake fluid reservoir caps have a small float attached to their undersides, which operates the low brake fluid level warning light, so allow the fluid to drain from the float back into the reservoir before lifting it out. Place the cap on a wad of clean cloth to catch any drips.

Top up with fresh brake fluid to bring the level up to the appropriate mark. If the filler cap has a float attached to it, bear in mind that the float will cause the fluid level to rise when you refit the cap.

When you've finished, carefully screw the cap tightly back into position and wipe up any spillage.

Coolant

The engine must be cold to check the coolant, so if you've driven the car recently, allow it to cool for a couple of hours first.

With the car parked on level ground, find the coolant reservoir, and check that the coolant level is up to the level indicated on the side, or between the 'MAX' and 'MIN' marks.

If the coolant needs topping up, place a wad of rag over the top of the filler cap and slowly unscrew the cap to release the pressure in the system. NEVER unscrew the filler cap if the engine is hot. Top up the level using a 50/50 mixture of clean water and antifreeze. When you've finished, refit the cap tightly and wipe away any spillage.

Windscreen wipers

Lift the wiper arm from the glass until it locks in the upright position. Wipe the cleaning edge of the blade using a clean cloth dipped in undiluted washer fluid.

Run a finger along the edge of the blade to check for damage. If there are any cracks or splits, fit a new blade.

135

Windscreen washer

It's a good idea to top up the windscreen washer reservoir every week. First wipe away any dirt from around the filler neck, then pull off the filler cap. Fill the reservoir with a mixture of washer fluid and clean water. Use a higher proportion of washer fluid in winter, as indicated by the directions on the bottle, to prevent the washer from freezing in cold weather.

Whenever you check the washer fluid level it's a good idea to check also that the washer jets are working. To do this, close the bonnet, switch on the ignition and operate the washers. You can clear a blocked washer jet by poking the nozzle gently with a pin. You can also use the pin to swivel the nozzle 'eyeball' so that the jet is correctly aimed. Aim the jets so that the washer fluid hits the windscreen slightly higher up than you want it, as the airflow will push the water downwards when the car is moving.

Battery

A quick battery check each week can help to avoid trouble – faulty battery connections and flat batteries are among the most common causes of breakdowns.

Check that the cable clamps are tight to ensure good connections – you shouldn't be able to move them. Also check the battery cables for cracks and fraying.

If the cable clamps are corroded (white fluffy deposits), clean them with a small wire brush. Corrosion can be prevented by spraying the terminals with battery terminal protector or smearing them with petroleum jelly.

Most modern batteries are maintenance-free and don't need to be topped up. Maintenance-free batteries usually have a condition indicator fitted, often a disc that changes colour to indicate the condition of the battery. Usually a green disc indicates that the battery is okay, and the disc darkens as the battery condition deteriorates. Check the battery instructions for details of how to use the indicator.

Use a wire brush to remove any corrosion on the battery terminals

Check that your car's tyres are inflated to the correct pressure – and don't forget the spare wheel

Tyres

Working on each wheel in turn, unscrew the tyre valve dust cap and put it somewhere safe. If any dust caps are missing, replace them.

Check the tyre pressure by pushing the nozzle of the gauge firmly onto the valve so that no air can be heard escaping. Check the reading on the gauge against the pressures recommended in your car's handbook. The pressures for front and rear tyres are often different, and if you're carrying a heavy load the pressures should be increased.

Tyre pressures need to be checked cold, which means that the car should not have been driven recently. Tyre pressures increase with temperature, so bear in mind that on a hot summer's day there can be a significant difference in the pressure reading for a tyre on the side of the car in the shade compared to that on the side in direct sunlight.

If the pressure needs increasing slightly, use a footpump to inflate the tyre, or drive the car to the nearest garage and use their air supply.

Then check the pressure again. If it's now too high, remove the gauge and gently press the pin in the centre of the tyre valve to release a small quantity of air. Re-check the pressure with the gauge. Refit the dust cap when you've finished.

Don't forget the spare tyre – it's a good idea to inflate this to the highest of the pressures suggested for your car.

All tyres must have at least the minimum legal amount of tread – that's 1.6 mm in the UK, although it's better to replace tyres well before they become this worn. Most tyres have tread wear indicator bars, or you can use a tyre tread depth gauge to check the depth.

At the same time, carry out a quick check on the condition of each tyre. Look for uneven tread wear damage, and also for bulges, or anything embedded in treads or sidewalls. If you find any problems it's a good idea to visit a tyre specialist and ask their advice.

Breakdowns

These are the ten most common causes of breakdowns – with tips on how to avoid them.

1) Flat or faulty battery
To avoid problems, check the battery terminals regularly, making sure they're secure and free from corrosion. If you make lots of short journeys, take your car on an occasional long journey to help the alternator charge the battery. Check the alternator drivebelt once in a while, and at the first sign of trouble, such as difficult starting, dim headlights, or if the charging warning light comes on, have the battery tested.

2) Flat or damaged tyres or wheels
Check the tyre pressures and the condition of the tyres regularly. Don't forget the spare. If you 'kerb' a wheel when parking or driving, check the condition of the wheel and tyre as soon as possible afterwards. In case of a puncture, consider carrying a can of tyre 'instant repair' foam, and make sure that the jack, wheel brace and removal tool for locking wheel bolts are in the car and that you know how to use them.

3) Alternator faults
The alternator's job is to charge the battery, and if it fails, the battery will soon fail too. The telltale signs of a problem are dim headlights when the engine is ticking over, a squealing sound from the engine compartment, which may indicate a slipping alternator drivebelt, and a glowing charging warning light, especially when the engine is ticking over. Stop as soon as possible if the charging warning light comes on when you're driving.

4) Starter motor failure
If you hear metallic noises when you try to start the engine, or there's a click from the engine compartment but the engine doesn't turn over, then it's likely that the starter motor has failed.

5) Ignition problems
In older cars fitted with a distributor cap, problems are indicated by misfiring of the engine, especially when accelerating or driving uphill, or difficulty starting the engine, especially in damp weather.

6) Running out of fuel or filling with the wrong fuel

Both of these problems are easily avoidable. Always keep an eye on your fuel gauge, and don't wait until the warning light comes on before filling up. If you're travelling on a road where fuel stations are scarce, ensure you have enough fuel to make it to the next large town. When driving an unfamiliar car, make sure you know what type of fuel it takes and that you've selected the correct fuel pump before starting to fill up.

7) Damage to clutch cables

If you have a manual gearbox and the clutch cable breaks, you won't be able to change gear – nothing will happen when you press the clutch pedal. Telltale signs of a problem include a strange feeling clutch action or if the gears crunch when changing gear. (The above doesn't apply to hydraulic clutches).

8) Neglected spark plugs

In petrol engines signs of a problem include engine misfiring when accelerating, and difficulty starting the engine, especially in damp weather. To help avoid problems, fit new spark plugs at the manufacturer's recommended intervals.

9) Faults with ignition HT leads

In some petrol engines the HT leads connect the spark plugs to the coil, and they deteriorate with age. To help to avoid problems, keep the HT leads clean and securely connected. Signs of a problem include engine misfiring when accelerating, and difficulty starting the engine, especially in damp weather.

10) Leaking cylinder head gasket

A leaking cylinder head gasket can be a big problem. A major cause is overheating, so check your car's temperature gauge, and if it creeps towards the red zone stop and check the coolant level. Signs of a problem include a lack of power, misfiring (especially when the engine is cold or when starting), fluid leaks on the outside of the engine, coolant in the oil (looks like frothy 'mayonnaise'), or a mysterious drop in coolant level and the need for frequent topping up.

Faulty batteries are the number one cause of breakdowns

Help yourself

Flat batteries and punctures are two of the most common causes of breakdowns. Learn how to jump start an engine and change a wheel, and you'll soon be on your way again.

Jump starting

If you have a flat battery, you can start the car by using jump leads to connect the flat battery to one in another vehicle. WARNING: Be wary jump starting cars with engine management systems as if the leads spark it can damage electronic components. If in doubt check your car's handbook or call a breakdown service.

First position the vehicles so that you can connect the batteries using the jump leads. Switch off the ignition and all electrical equipment on both vehicles, make sure handbrakes are on, and gears are in neutral (or 'P' on an automatic).

Connect one end of the red jump lead to the positive (+) terminal of the flat battery. Don't let the other end of the jump lead touch any metal. Then connect the other end of the red lead to the positive (+) terminal of the fully charged battery.

Connect one end of the black jump lead to the negative (–) terminal of the fully-charged battery, then connect the other end of the lead to a metal bolt or bracket well away from the battery on the engine block of the vehicle to be started.

Make sure that that the jump leads can't come into contact with any moving parts on either engine, then start the vehicle with the fully-charged battery and run it at a fast tickover. Next start the engine of the vehicle with the flat battery, and make sure that it's running properly.

Stop the engine of the vehicle with the fully charged battery, then disconnect the jump leads. Disconnect the black lead first – from the vehicle with the flat battery, and then from the vehicle with the fully charged battery; then disconnect the red lead – from the vehicle with the fully charged battery first, then from the vehicle with the flat battery.

It will take some time for the alternator to charge the flat battery, so take it for a drive and don't stop the engine too soon.

Take care to connect the leads correctly when jump starting a car with a flat battery

It's worth practising how to change a wheel at home so you know what to do if you get a flat tyre on the road

Changing a wheel

Changing a wheel is straightforward, but if you've just bought the car, or if you've never changed a wheel before, it's worth practising at home so you'll know exactly what to do if you get a flat tyre.

First check that the car is parked on level ground, and make sure that the handbrake is applied. Select first gear (manual transmission) or 'P' (automatic transmission).

Get out the spare wheel, car jack and wheel brace. Chock the wheel diagonally opposite the one to be changed, using a couple of wooden blocks or large stones.

Pull off the wheel trim, if fitted, then use the wheelbrace to loosen each wheel bolt (or nut) on the affected wheel by about half a turn.

Engage the jack head in the jacking point nearest the affected wheel (check your car's handbook to locate it). As a safety measure, slide the spare wheel part way under the side of the car, near the wheel to be removed, but out of the way of the jack. Raise the jack until the wheel is a few centimetres off the ground.

Remove the wheel bolts, and lift off the wheel. Drag the spare wheel out from under the side of the car, and slide the removed wheel under the car in its place.

Fit the spare wheel, then refit the bolts, and tighten them until they're just holding the wheel firmly.

Remove the wheel from under the car, then lower the jack and take it away it from under the car.

Tighten one wheel bolt securely, using the wheelbrace, then tighten the one diagonally opposite. Tighten the other two bolts in the same way, then refit the wheel trim.

When you've finished, stow the removed wheel and the tools back in their correct locations. Check the pressure in the newly-fitted tyre.

Remember to get the flat tyre repaired or renewed as soon as possible, so that you have a spare if you're unlucky enough to get a second puncture.

Troubleshooting

Modern cars are now more reliable, but it's useful to know what can go wrong.

If your car won't start

Before calling for help, run through the following checks, just in case you can fix the problem yourself.

- Is the immobiliser on? Check that you know how it works, and make sure that you know the starting procedure.
- On automatic transmissions the engine won't start unless the selector lever is in the 'N' or 'P' position.
- If there is no starter motor sound (or just a clicking noise), then the starter motor may be faulty, or the battery flat.
- You could just be out of fuel (the gauge may be faulty).
- Some petrol-engined cars have a cut-off switch that stops the fuel flow in the event of an accident. Sometimes this switch can be triggered by a pothole or a minor bump and has to be reset manually – check your car's handbook for details, and try resetting it.
- On some cars you need to depress the clutch before starting the engine (check the handbook for information).

If your car stops unexpectedly

If the engine stops suddenly, causes can include:

- a faulty ignition switch.
- loose wires or connections in the ignition system.
- a loose battery earth.
- broken ignition components.

If the engine splutters or misfires, then loses power and stops, you should consider these possible causes:

- empty fuel tank.
- fuel cut-off switch activated (petrol models).
- dirt or water in fuel lines.
- damp ignition components.
- faulty ignition system components.

If the engine makes unpleasant noises then stops, it indicates a more serious mechanical failure, such as a broken timing belt.

Warning lights

All cars are fitted with warning lights to alert the driver to possible faults. Some warnings are more serious than others, so here's a guide to what the more common warning lights mean, and what to do if they come on. All the warning lights are usually explained in the car's handbook.

Warning light   **What it means**

Low brake fluid level/worn brake pads:
Check the brake fluid level and top up if necessary. If the level is low, have the car checked for brake fluid leaks, and don't drive it until it is fixed. If pads are worn, have them checked as soon as possible.

Alternator isn't charging battery: The car can be driven, but not too far, as the battery may eventually go flat. Have the alternator and its wiring checked as soon as possible.

Oil pressure too low: If the light comes on when driving, stop the engine immediately, check the oil level and look for leaks, then call for assistance. Serious and expensive damage could be caused if you carry on running the engine.

Coolant temperature too high or coolant level too low: Stop as soon as possible, allow the engine to cool, then check the coolant level. Top up if necessary. If the light comes on again, get assistance.

Engine system warning: The car can be driven, but it may lack performance. Have it checked as soon as possible.

Diesel glow plug warning: This is normal, just wait for the light to go out before starting the engine.

ABS warning: The car can be driven, but the ABS may not be working (normal braking won't be affected). Have the ABS tested as soon as possible.

Airbag system fault: The car can be driven, but the airbag system may not work. Have the airbag system checked as soon as possible.

Handbrake is on: Check the handbrake is released if you're about to drive off.

Fluid leaks

A leak may show up as a stain under your car, or you may be forever topping up one of the fluids. So how do you tell if a leak is serious, or something you can live with for a while?

- Petrol has a strong, distinctive smell, so a leak should be obvious. If you've just filled up with petrol on a hot day, liquid or vapour may leak out through the fuel tank breather. Petrol can also leak if you park a car with a full tank on a steep slope. If the leak isn't due to either of these causes, have it investigated straight away. Don't drive the car until the leak's been fixed.

- Diesel fuel has a distinctive oily smell. As with petrol, a recently filled tank may leak a little due to expansion. Any other leak is a cause for concern. Don't drive the car until the leak's been fixed.

- Engine oil is usually black. The most common sources of leaks are the oil drain plug, the oil filter, and the sump gasket under the engine. You can drive with a minor oil leak, but keep an eye on the oil level.

- Coolant is usually brightly coloured, with a strong, sickly sweet smell. Leaks usually come from a hose, the radiator, or the heater (you'll smell coolant when you turn the heater on). You can drive with a minor leak, but if you lose too much coolant, the engine could overheat.

- Brake/clutch hydraulic fluid is clear and thin. Brake fluid leaks usually come from the brake master cylinder or reservoir, but may also appear around the wheels or the brake line connections under the car. Clutch fluid leaks usually come from hydraulic line connections, or from failed seals. Don't drive the car if you think there might be a brake fluid leak. It's fine to drive with a minor clutch fluid leak, but if you lose all the fluid the clutch won't work.

If you need to keep topping up fluid, it probably means there's a leak

- Manual transmission or final drive oil is usually a tan colour or reddish-pink. Transmission oil is thicker than engine oil, and often has a very sickly smell, especially when hot. You can drive with a minor leak, but if the oil level gets too low it can cause serious transmission damage.
- Automatic transmission fluid may be clear or reddish-brown. Leaks usually come from the transmission casing, or from fluid lines running to the fluid cooler. You can drive with a minor leak, but keep an eye on the fluid level.
- Power steering fluid is clear or reddish-brown. Leaks usually come from fluid line connections, the power steering pump, or the steering gear. You can drive with a minor leak, but keep an eye on the fluid level.
- Shock absorber fluid usually shows up as a dark stain on the shock absorber body. You can drive the car, but it may have a poor ride and poor handling – so take care!
- Grease is usually black or grey, thick, and very sticky! You may find it under the car if it has leaked from the driveshaft rubber gaiters or steering gear gaiters. You can drive the car, but if much grease has been lost the driveshaft or steering gear could be damaged.
- Washer fluid usually contains a coloured dye, and has a strong smell of detergent, alcohol or ammonia. A leak could be due to a poor pipe connection, or a leaky washer pump seal in the fluid reservoir.
- Water on the ground beneath your car may not be a leak but simply condensation from the air conditioning.

Engine overheating

Overheating is a serious problem. When the engine gets hot, the cooling fan should cut in to lower the temperature. If the temperature gauge stays in the red, don't be tempted to carry on driving – stop as soon as possible. (As an emergency measure, turning the heater blower onto full speed and selecting maximum heat will bring the temperature down a little.) Causes of overheating include low coolant level, faulty cooling fan, coolant leakage, a faulty coolant pump or a broken coolant pump drivebelt.

Fuel problems

If you run out of fuel, don't keep on trying to start the engine. You'll suck air, and maybe dirt from the empty tank, into the fuel system, which will make starting harder once you've filled up.

If you have a can of fuel, switch off the ignition and empty it in the tank. Operate the starter for short bursts, and if the engine starts, drive on and fill the tank at the next fuel station. If the engine still won't start, dirt or air drawn into the fuel system could be causing problems, and you'll need to get help.

145

Running out of fuel can cause problems, so try to fill up before the warning light comes on

On diesel-engined cars, if you've run out of fuel the engine may be difficult to start even when you've refilled the tank, because of air being drawn into the fuel lines. Most cars are fitted with a hand priming pump, normally a large pushbutton on top of the fuel filter. Switch on the ignition, then pump the priming button until you feel resistance indicating that the air has been expelled. Try to start the engine with the accelerator fully depressed. If it still won't start, air has probably been drawn into the fuel injection pump, and you'll need help.

And what should you do if you fill up with the wrong fuel? Firstly, don't turn on the ignition or the fuel pump may start up with damaging consequences. If you have put in a large amount of the wrong fuel – over five litres – then you need to call for help to have the fuel system drained and cleaned. If you put in only a small amount, then top up with the right fuel and you should get away with it – though check that doing so won't invalidate your car's warranty.

Smoky exhaust

A short burst of white smoke from the exhaust when you start the car first thing in the morning is no problem – it's just condensation from the exhaust turning into steam. Many diesel engines puff out black smoke if you accelerate hard – again, it's nothing to worry about. Diesel engines also produce a certain amount of white smoke when starting up, especially in cold weather. If it seems to be excessive, have the glow plugs checked. More worrying is:

- ◯ White smoke caused by coolant getting into the cylinders, probably from a leaking cylinder head gasket. On turbocharged engines, white smoke could be due to a leaking oil seal in the turbo. Have the problem checked out immediately, or the turbocharger may fail quickly.
- ◯ Bluish-white smoke is caused by an oil leak inside the engine, normally due to worn valve-stem oil seals inside the cylinder head (not a huge problem), or worn engine bearings or cylinder bores (more serious).

◐ Black smoke is normally caused by too much fuel in the air/fuel mixture (this can damage the catalytic converter, so don't drive the car any further than you have to).

Strange noises

An unusual noise could just be an irritating distraction, or it may spell more serious trouble.

◐ **Noises from the exhaust**

A puffing or blowing noise indicates a hole or crack in the exhaust system; a rattle or thumping over bumps points to a loose or broken exhaust mounting.

◐ **Noises from the brakes**

Light squeaking from the brakes is usually nothing to worry about, but a harsh metallic scraping means the pads could be worn out. A chattering noise when the brakes are applied indicates contaminated brake pads and needs checking.

◐ **Noises from the suspension**

Clunks or rattles may indicate worn or damaged suspension components. A rumbling or clicking when turning corners points to worn wheel bearings or driveshaft joints, while a hissing sound over bumps indicates worn shock absorbers.

◐ **Noises from the engine**

A rhythmic slapping from a cold engine is piston slap, which should go away once warm. A metallic thudding points to more serious worn engine bearings or camshaft, while a light tapping from the top of the engines indicates that the valve clearances need checking or possibly a worn camshaft. A metallic rattling under acceleration is 'pinking', caused by poor fuel or an ignition fault.

◐ **Noises from the transmission**

A whine or howl when the gearbox is in neutral indicates a worn transmission bearing; if this noise is heard when the clutch is depressed, the clutch release bearing is likely to be at fault. Squealing as the clutch is engaged points to a worn or badly adjusted clutch. A graunching when changing gear can mean the clutch needs adjusting, or that the gearbox synchromesh is worn.

Don't ignore noisy brakes – they may be badly worn and need replacing

For a car to be reliable it must be properly serviced. Regular maintenance isn't going to prevent every possible failure, but it will minimise the risk of your car letting you down.

Every car manufacturer specifies a service schedule for each of its models, and it's important to make sure that this schedule is followed. If servicing is neglected, it's almost inevitable that sooner or later your car will suffer the consequences, which could prove inconvenient, expensive, or both!

If you have the service record book that was originally supplied with your car when it was new, this should contain a service schedule. If you don't have a service schedule, an authorised dealer for your make of car should be able to provide you with one.

Whether you have the servicing carried out by a garage, or whether you decide to do it yourself, is a matter of personal choice. DIY servicing will certainly save you money, but you may not have the experience, confidence, or enthusiasm to carry out all the servicing yourself.

Typical service schedule

Every 12 months or 20,000 miles – whichever comes first:
- Check indicators and lights.
- Check windscreen and headlamp wash/wipe system.
- Renew engine oil and filter.
- Check coolant level.
- Check brake fluid level.
- Check power steering fluid level.
- Check automatic transmission fluid level.
- Check auxiliary drivebelts.
- Check clutch pedal adjustment.
- Renew fuel filter (petrol engines).
- Check handbrake adjustment.
- Check suspension components.
- Check brake pipes and hoses.
- Check fuel lines.
- Check exhaust system.
- Check front and rear brake components.
- Check transmission for leaks.
- Check air conditioning compressor for leaks.
- Check steering rubber gaiters.

- Check track rod ends and driveshaft gaiters.
- Check wheel bolt torque and tyre pressures.
- Check headlight alignment.
- Lubricate door hinges, door stops, locks, bonnet release and tailgate hinges.

Every 12 months, regardless of mileage:
- Drain water from the fuel filter (diesel engines).
- Check body and underbody for damage.

Every 20,000 miles, regardless of time interval:
- Renew fuel filter.

Every two years, regardless of mileage:
- Replace batteries in the central-locking remote control.
- Renew brake fluid.

Every two years or 20,000 miles – whichever comes first:
- Renew pollen filter.

Every four years or 40,000 miles – whichever comes first:
- Renew air cleaner element.
- Renew spark plugs (petrol engines).
- Renew automatic transmission fluid.
- Remove brake drums and check and clean brake shoe components.

Every eight years or 80,000 miles – whichever comes first:
- Replace timing belt and pulleys (it's advisable to replace these components more frequently for many models).

Regular servicing is essential to keep a car running safely and reliably

DIY servicing

Carrying out your own servicing can be satisfying, as well as money-saving. Because the steps involved in a specific service procedure vary so much from car to car, information for each and every servicing task can't be included here. You'll find all the information you need for servicing procedures specific to your car in the relevant Haynes Manual.

Safety first

If you're going to carry out any work on your car, your first priority must always be safety.

It's a sensible precaution to wear disposable gloves, as this will protect your hands and will make it a lot easier to clean them afterwards.

If you're working under the bonnet and the engine has run recently, remember that some engine components, particularly the exhaust system, can be hot enough to cause serious burns.

Tools

A selection of basic tools is essential. The tool kit supplied with most cars won't allow you to do much more than change a wheel! You don't need the most expensive tools, but generally you get what you pay for, and a good quality set will last years.

Engine oil and filter change

One relatively straightforward servicing task you may like to tackle for yourself is changing the oil and oil filter.

It's not uncommon for oil change intervals these days to be as long as 20,000 miles. In spite of this, it's a good idea to change the oil more frequently than the manufacturer recommends. Oil deteriorates with age, so you should always change it once a year even if you drive very few miles.

To change the oil you'll need plenty of clean cloth, disposable gloves, a draining container (usually about five litres in capacity), an oil filter removal tool, a spanner or drain plug key, a new oil filter, a new oil drain plug sealing washer, a pack of engine oil of the correct type, and a funnel.

The car should be parked on level ground and the engine should be warm. Remove the oil filler cap from the top of the engine. Slacken the drain plug in the sump beneath the engine using the spanner or drain plug key. Unscrew it by hand the last couple of turns, keeping the plug pressed into its hole. When the plug comes out, pull it away quickly so that the oil runs straight into the container. Wipe the drain plug clean, then remove the old sealing washer and fit the new one.

Allow about ten minutes for the oil to drain. When the oil stops draining, wipe around the drain plug hole, then screw in the plug and tighten it.

Remove the drain plug in the oil sump using a spanner or drain plug key

Next, reposition the draining container underneath the oil filter, then use the oil filter removal tool to slacken the filter. Once the filter is loose, unscrew it by hand. Drain the oil from inside the filter into the container. Wipe clean the filter mounting on the engine. Take the new oil filter and, using your finger, smear a little clean engine oil on the rubber sealing ring.

Screw on the new filter until the sealing ring touches, then tighten it by hand about another half to three-quarters of a turn. Remove the draining container and pour the old oil into a container to take to your local oil recycling centre.

Check your car's handbook to see how much oil the engine needs, then pour in about two-thirds of this through the filler hole. Wait a few minutes for the oil to drain down into the engine, then pull out the dipstick and check the oil level. Keep topping up the oil and re-checking the level until the level reaches the upper mark on the dipstick, then refit the filler cap.

Start the engine. The red oil pressure warning light on the instrument panel may take a few seconds to go out – if it doesn't go out, stop the engine! Run the engine for a few minutes and check for leaks around the oil filter and drain plug. Re-tighten slightly if necessary, but don't overtighten.

Stop the engine and wait a few minutes for the oil to run down into the sump again, then re-check the oil level. Top up if necessary, but don't overfill.

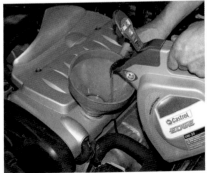

Top up with fresh oil, but take care not to overfill the engine

All cars over three years old must by law pass an annual health check – the MoT test.

You won't be able to carry out all the checks that feature in the MoT test at home, but working through the following checks may help you to spot possible problems and get them fixed before taking the car for its test.

Brakes

Check that the handbrake works correctly and can't be released by tapping the lever sideways. If you have to pull the lever up a long way the cables probably need adjustment.

Press on the brake pedal and check it doesn't move down as far as the floor. If the pedal feels spongy, this probably means that there's air in the hydraulic system which must be removed by bleeding. Check the brake servo unit by pushing the brake pedal several times, then keep it pushed down while starting the engine. As the engine starts the pedal should move down slightly – if not, the servo may be faulty.

Look under the bonnet and check all the brake components, brake pipes and servo for leaks, loose mountings, or corrosion. The fluid reservoir must be secure and the fluid level correct.

Steering wheel and column

Check that the steering wheel is not loose, and that there's no abnormal movement that would indicate wear in the column or its joints.

Windscreen, mirrors and sun visor

The windscreen must be free from cracks and other damage within the driver's field of vision (small stone chips will not cause an MoT failure). All rear-view mirrors must be secure, undamaged and capable of being adjusted. The driver's sun visor must be capable of being stored in the 'up' position.

Doors

Both front doors must be able to be opened and closed from the outside and inside, with the car at rest, and must latch securely when closed.

Exhaust system

With the engine running, hold a cloth over the exhaust tailpipe. If there are no leaks, the engine will stall after a few seconds.

Seat belts and seats

Inspect the webbing of all the seat belts for cuts and fraying. Check the buckles work properly, and check the retracting mechanism. The front seats must be securely attached, and the backrests must lock securely in the upright position.

Electrical items

Ensure that the horn, windscreen wipers and washers work. On cars fitted with ABS and airbags, the warning lights should illuminate when the ignition is switched on, and then go out after a few seconds.

Check the operation of all the lights, including the brake lights and number plate light, and check that the lenses and reflectors are clean and undamaged. Check the condition of the wiper blades, and renew damaged or perished blades.

Steering and suspension

Press down on each corner of the car then release it. The body should move back to its original position and settle. If it bounces, or you hear hissing, the shock absorber is worn or faulty.

Turn the steering wheel slightly from side to side, up to the point where the road wheels just begin to move. Make sure that there's no excessive free play between the steering wheel and the road wheels, which would indicate worn steering components. If your car has power steering, check that the pump is secure and free from leaks, and check the power steering fluid reservoir, hoses and pipes for leaks.

Vehicle identification

The number plates must be in good condition, securely fitted, and easily readable, with letters and numbers correctly spaced.

A shock absorber which has seized will cause the car to fail the MoT

Most new cars have a high standard of security, but there are still measures you can take to prevent yours falling victim to a car thief.

Simple security measures

In the majority of car crimes, the car is broken into or stolen in a very short space of time, with little force or effort required. Apart from using security devices, there are several common-sense steps you can take to make life harder for would-be criminals:

- Always lock your car – even in the garage or driveway at home, or at a filling station if you've just filled up with fuel and are popping into the kiosk to pay. Many modern cars have anti-theft deadlocks – if your car has them, make sure you always activate them when locking your car. Don't forget to lock the fuel filler (if it has a separate lock), and if the car's in the garage, lock the garage. If your car is stolen or broken into while it's unlocked, your insurance company may not pay out.

- Always remove the ignition key – even in the garage or driveway at home.

- Close all the windows and the sunroof – if a window or sunroof is open, you're making a criminal's job much easier. A door can be opened much more quickly with the aid of an open window.

- Park in a visible location – if possible, always try to park in an attended car park, and in a space where your car is highly visible. If you have to park at night, in a car park or at the roadside, try to pick a well-lit area (under a street light, for instance).

- Never leave valuable items on display – if you can't take it with you, lock it in the boot. Don't leave valuable items in the glovebox. Don't leave your vehicle documents in the car, as they could help a thief to sell it.

- If your car has a telescopic radio aerial, put it down when parking – alternatively, you can have a telescopic aerial replaced with a less vulnerable flexible rubber one.

- Protect in-car entertainment (ICE) equipment. Most modern equipment is security-coded, and won't work if it's disconnected from the battery. If your equipment has a removable panel, make sure you remove this when you leave the car.

Security equipment

Most modern cars have immobilisers and alarm systems as standard equipment, and many also have the glass etched with the registration number or VIN number. Most insurance companies give a discount for cars fitted with an immobiliser and/or alarm system.

If your car doesn't have any security equipment, consider some or all of the following:

- Have an immobiliser fitted – electronic immobilisers will prevent the engine from being started, and mechanical devices such as steering wheel and gear lever locks can act as a visible deterrent.

- Consider having an alarm fitted. The best alarms are expensive, but they will deter thieves. Many alarms have built in immobilisers, and it's even possible to fit a tracking system that will allow the police to monitor the movement of a stolen car. Fitting an alarm system can be a tricky job, as it means tapping in to the car's electrical system, so it's wise to have it professionally fitted.

- Have your car windows etched with the registration number or Vehicle Identification Number – this will help to trace your car if it's stolen and the thieves try to change its identity. Other glass components such as sunroofs and headlights can also be etched. Many garages and windscreen specialists provide this service.

- Use locking wheel nuts. If your car has alloy wheels, always fit locking wheel nuts to deter thieves. Alloy wheels are the first item on many thieves' shopping lists!

There are a number of simple security measures you can take to make a car thief think twice about trying to break into your car

Whatever your area of interest, Haynes have got it covered...

From car service and repair manuals covering 95% of cars on the roads today, to techbooks and restoration manuals...

...service and repair manuals for motorcycles ranging from superbikes to scooters and motorcycle techbooks...

...books for cyclists feature *The Bike Book* and *Mountain Biking Skills*...

...books for the home including the *Washing Machine Manual*, *Loft Conversion Manual* and home repairs...

...books for travelling, including *The Caravan Manual* and *Driving Abroad* and, last but not least, books for reading and enjoying...

...Motorsport biographies, Formula 1, motorcycling, classic cars, and much, much more...